Your Child's Vision:

A Parent's Guide to Seeing, Growing, and Developing

Richard S. Kavner, O.D.

Illustrations by Felice Gittleman

Simon and Schuster
New York

Copyright © 1985 by Richard Kavner, O.D.

Published by Simon and Schuster
A Division of Simon & Schuster, Inc.
Simon & Schuster Building
Rockefeller Center
1230 Avenue of the Americas
New York, New York 10020

SIMON AND SCHUSTER and colophon are
registered trademarks of Simon & Schuster, Inc.

Designed by H. Roberts Design

Manufactured in the United States of America

10 9 8 7 6 5 4 3 2 1

Library of Congress Cataloging in Publication Data

Kavner, Richard S.
  Your child's vision.

  "A Fireside book."
  Bibliography: p.
  Includes index.
  1. Vision disorders in children. 2. Visual
perception in children. 3. Vision disorders in
children—complications and sequelae.   I. Title.
  RE48.2.C5K38   1985   618.92'0977   85-1859

ISBN: 0-671-55449-2

This book is dedicated to Saul, Gertie, and Mike—
for a love that was always available and everlasting.

Acknowledgments

I am indebted to many people:

To Dr. A.M. Skeffington and his associates for opening my eyes;

to all the people at the Gesell Institute for Child Development for their insights into Visual Development and Children's Behavior;

to the many people who helped me to clarify my ideas: Dr. Charles Margach, Dr. Gerald Getman, Dr. Harold Solan, Dr. Amiel Francke, Dr. Bennett Roth, Dr. Virginia Pomeranz, Dr. John Diamond, Dr. Ben Lane;

to my mother, Sylvia Kavner, for her constant support and sketches on pages 133, 136, 137, and 157;

to my editors: Angela Miller, who first nudged me on my way; Charles Rue Woods, who didn't let me stray; Kendra Crossen, for straightening out my prose;

to my sons, Teddy and Billy, for the pleasure they give me as I watch them grow, and for their patience and understanding when I can't come out to play;

and finally, to my wife, Carole, for the many hours of help, support, encouragement, criticism, and love. This book would be incomplete without her presence.

Contents

Foreword

My first exposure to the field of developmental optometry took place in 1975. I was familiar with the Gesell Institute in New Haven and their dedication to studies of childhood development; but I had no idea how far their thinking and experimentation—inspired to a substantial degree by the observations and writings of the renowned Swiss psychologist Jean Piaget—had moved into the area of vision and visual-motor function. The first patient whom I witnessed being examined by means of the refined methods of visual analysis was a young woman in her early twenties who had struggled, for nearly ten years, to overcome an illness that had been diagnosed as psychiatric. In the course of the examination, I discovered, to my astonishment, that she was functionally blind, and had probably been so since childhood. Even more amazing was the fact that a six-month program of visual training, combined with special prisms to "expand the visual space around her," enabled her to use her visual systems effectively and to resume the normal activities of work, friendship, marriage, and eventually motherhood, none of which seemed remotely possible during her long interlude of illness and psychiatric treatment. The young woman was my daughter.

Since then, in collaboration with developmental optometrists such as Dr. Richard Kavner, the author of this book, Dr. William Moskowitz, and Dr. Melvin Kaplan, I have observed varying degrees of visual-perceptual dysfunction in a substantial number of psychiatric patients. Treatment has led to considerably improved social, occupational, and academic performance, thereby helping them recover from their various states of emotional disability. I now consider the analysis of visual function an inherent part of any complete medical-psychiatric evaluation.

At the same time, many of my concepts about the nature of so-called mental illness have changed as well. We psychiatrists have a professional dictionary of diagnostic terms. We call it Diagnostic Statistical Manual—III. It permits us to communicate more effectively with each other about various patients. It protects us against the chaos that would result from a total lack of definition. It enables us to fill out health insurance forms. But it has also become a straightjacket, easily misused to categorize patients and place them into artificially constructed little compartments that carry with them terrifying stigma. Too often, an official diagnosis can become a patient's ruthless destiny. Terms such as schizophrenia have too often come to imply that an individual is suffering with some well-understood illness, prone to go on forever and for which only palliative treatment measures are available, when, in fact, there may not really be any such thing as schizophrenia.

The static concepts of mental health and illness that still pervade our thinking are consistent with a simplistic viewpoint toward human experience put forth by a number of psychiatrists and behavioral scientists, including Sigmund Freud himself, whose theories predated modern visions of the universe offered us by Einstein, deChardin, and others. The human being is anything but static. We are always in a state of flux, part of open systems in which cycles of disruption and reintegration are inherent ingredients of being alive. What we call illness can better be seen as a failure to transit necessary periods of disruption. What we call health can better be viewed as psychobiological resilience, a wholeness of body, mind, spirit, and environment that permits us to move through episodes of change, of falling apart and spontanously putting ourselves and our worlds back together again, toward a new and higher level of equilibrium, periodically throughout life.

Effective vision—and, after all, vision is one of the key routes whereby information is processed to the brain—must be seen as part of such resilience, playing a vital role in maintaining and restoring mental health.

More than that—visual perception is obviously a critical factor in the learning process, not just the acquisition of facts but the very nature of learning and thinking itself. Piaget made this distinction beautifully when he differentiated between knowledge and knowing. Having information at your fingertips is one thing. It may help you do well in your college entrance examinations, if you can see well enough to find the box to check next to the answers in each multiple choice question. But it is far from enough to help you achieve in college, once you've been accepted, or master the skills and challenges of whatever career you choose, or effectively handle your interpersonal relationships. To meet these opportunities and demands, you must be creative—able to engage in divergent as well as convergent thinking, to forfeit obsolete ways of "viewing" things in favor of new and better ways when the situation calls for it. My son, Christopher, now completing his Ph.D. thesis in psychology, is studying that very point— whether visual perceptual style influences the degree to which a person can use his or her creative abilities. Personally, I believe it does, profoundly so.

What all this adds up to is Dr. Kavner's book, a clear and concise presentation of visual function, tactics parents can use to encourage healthy function in their children, clues which they can fall back on to identify the possibility of visual perceptual disabilities requiring diagnosis and treatment. It should be self-evident to most readers that visual problems are really quite common and that their recognition and correction are quite feasible. Unfortunately, I never cease to be surprised at how common parental denial is. I used to think it applied largely to emotional and behavioral problems. It doesn't. A recommendation as nonthreatening as an eye examination—by a professional trained in developmental optometry!—often goes unheeded; sometimes, for reasons that defy even my experienced understanding, it is openly rejected. Why school systems do not routinely screen pupils for these problems baffles me as well. I can only say that those of you who read Dr. Kavner's book and take it seriously are most fortunate. No. Not you, really... your children will be the lucky ones.

Frederic F. Flach, M.D.
Cornell University Medical College
Payne Whitney Clinic of New York Hospital
St. Vincent's Hospital and Medical Center

Preface

We have all heard the commonplace statement that our sight is a precious gift, and most of us, as children, were cautioned frequently by our elders not to "ruin our eyes." Yet oddly enough, few seem to realize just how important vision is to our lives. Many people think of vision as synonymous with the eyeballs, which they regard as simply a marvelous pair of cameras. In thinking of vision this way, they fail to acknowledge the factors of intelligence and feeling that influence, and are influenced by, the sense of sight. In writing this book, my chief aim has been to demonstrate how extensively the quality of vision affects a child's growth—intellectually, emotionally, behaviorally, and socially.

Good vision does much more than simply enable a child to see the traffic lights when crossing the street, or what a teacher is writing on the board. It helps him or her to lead a fully dimensional life, with all the depth of understanding, breadth of feeling, and height of experience that this implies. Seeing, more than any other sense, guides and shapes your child's behavior and experience of life. You can understand, then, why I emphasize that to care for your child's vision is to care for his or her total development.

In the last decade science has learned what wise men and women have known for centuries—that our eyes are active seekers of the essence of life, not just passive, cameralike instruments. We know now that eyes are constantly searching, scanning, and selecting from the environment the important things to look at. The retina, we have learned, is not a tissue designed like a piece of film, but is instead a sophisticated network of interactive computers. The eye is a living organ that is always in communication with other vital centers of the body. What we think and how we feel are constant companions of the images we pay attention to. What we see depends not only upon what there is to look at, but also on what we feel we *should* see and what we think it should look like.

This partnership between our eyes and the rest of our body and mind matures as we actively experience and use our vision. In the first part of this book, I explore the stages of visual development, from birth to age five, and how they provide different themes for human growth. As development proceeds along its planned course, there are many byways that allow for the individual differences that we observe in children. The developmental plan allows for differences in direction and rate, giving us a chance to explore the nuances that are inherent in different environments, families, and cultures. In other words, the "melody" of development is the same for all children, but individual variations can alter the key. Thus, in Part One, I introduce the reader not only to the stages of visual development but also to the effects that each stage can have on the development of intelligence, social behavior, and the emotions.

Most of us, when we think of vision, think chiefly of the information that concerns the clarity of shapes in the environment. But long before visual mechanisms are used for seeing shapes, they are used to orient the child's body to the environment. A significant amount of information that we receive visually is concerned with what our bodies are doing in space. Without this information, we would have trouble maintaining an upright, graceful posture and coordinating our bodies when we reach for things or move through space. Posture, coordination, and balance—guided by vision—are important in a broad range of activities, from walking to catching a fly ball.

Besides providing information about objects in space and our orientation in space, vision helps the body to regulate glandular and hormonal activity. Scientists have come to recognize that there is a connection between the eyes and the centers in the brain that control biochemical functions. For example, some studies suggest that there is a relationship between the type and the amount of light that strikes the retina and reproductive development.

In the realm of emotion, literature abounds with references to the eyes as conveyors of love, and indeed vision helps the child experience the give and take of love in subtle ways—in the affection or encouragement reflected in a glance, for example, or in the sight of a smile slowly spreading its glow of warmth. These are some of the themes I wish to introduce in this book.

In Part Two, I examine the role that vision plays in the child's environment of school, home, and play areas. Among the significant issues covered here are learning disabilities related to vision, the effects of television viewing and the use of video display terminals, the visual skills and safety needs involved in sports, the selection of toys for promoting visual development, and the importance of good nutrition to good vision.

In Part Three, I discuss the different things that can go wrong with a child's vision, what causes them, and how they can be prevented or identified and treated. Again, the emphasis here is on treating the child as a whole person, not just as a pair of eyes, for if we attempt to improve or correct the eyes without considering the whole person, we risk creating further problems, with disastrous results. These new problems appear in physical, emotional, and intellectual disturbances that may not be recognized as related to the original eye problem. I have therefore devoted the final chapter to telling you how to find a good behavioral optometrist and what to expect when you take your child for an examination.

PART ONE:

VISION DEVELOPMENT

*Learning to see, learning to talk, learning to love
all take place in a little round schoolhouse called
earth.*

—George B. Leonard, *Education and Ecstasy*

I
The Infant: Birth to Eighteen Months

THE FIRST THREE MONTHS

And God said, "Let there be light"; and there
was light. And God saw that the light was
good; and God separated the light from the
darkness. God called the light Day, and the
darkness he called Night. And there was
evening and there was morning, the first day.

—Genesis 1:3–5

"I love you, Mommy."

Birth is but the first of many beginnings that your child will experience throughout his or her life. For parents, the birth of their child is an occasion for intense excitement and satisfaction, the culmination of nine months of building anticipation. For the child, however, birth is a great shock. Since conception, the child has lived in a protected environment with all of his needs supplied. Now, the child finds himself thrust into an alien world to which he must immediately begin to adapt in order to survive. And, as if following a preprogrammed set of instructions, the child does adapt to his new world in a manner that is so natural and appropriate that we take it for granted, unless something goes wrong.

If you take a closer look at the various stages of your child's development, you will become aware of an exquisite orchestration of processes that are taking place. Development may be viewed, in a sense, as an ever-expanding spiral. As your child moves along the widening turns of the spiral, there will occur a return to various developmental themes that were explored before, but each time they are experienced it is with a broader perspective, with new knowledge, new skills, and greater independence of action. This is evident when you watch your child learn to coordinate his body parts. At about four months of age, you can observe him thrashing about in the crib without evident purpose to his movements, but by six months the ability to roll over to the left or right has been achieved and you can see him practicing this skill with obvious delight. At eight months the efforts at coordination take on the new dimension of moving through space as your child learns to creep on the floor. This ability is further expanded as he learns to move about while standing up, at approximately fourteen months of age. At four years, the opposite sides of the body can be deftly coordinated for the purpose of walking down steps, and somewhere around six years you can observe and share in the thrill of his learning to master the coordination necessary to ride a two-wheel bicycle.

Each phase of the development of body coordination was dependent on, and involved refinement of, what had been learned before. The same pattern occurs in many other aspects of a child's development, particularly in his social, emotional, and visual development. Each of these areas has the opportunity to be explored and then dealt with at successively later ages, at which times integration with other skills occurs. The result is a finely interwoven mesh of abilities that the child can explore from different vantage points in time, at varied levels of interest, and with an ever-growing base of knowledge about the world.

The next time you go for a walk, notice how people navigate through mazes of streets, how they negotiate curves and wend their ways among other people and automobiles, without losing track of where they are or where they're going. Try to visualize the developmental steps that were required to arrive at this sophisticated level of behavior. It seems awesome, and it is! Yet, over the next few years, your own newborn baby will demonstrate development in each of these skills, which will improve, little by little, until the entire sophisticated process has become integrated and is automatic. The whole thrust of development, it appears, is learning mastery of self and of situations so as to function as an independent person.

It is interesting to see how the child's visual abilities often lead the way in this developmental scheme. The eyes act like searchlights, probing and illuminating the new terrain. In fact, the eyes are so important to this process that the pattern of development includes preparation while your child is still in the womb for the role his eyes will later play. About six months before being born, your baby was practicing the eye movements that would enable him to begin examining his environment very soon after birth. This ability to actively examine the environment is so intimately connected to growth and development that without it, normal development could actually cease to occur.

The first three months after birth is a period of incredible change for a baby and, not surprisingly, nature has seen to it that all the mechanisms necessary for survival are present. To be prepared for being thrust abruptly into his new, cold, and unprotected environment, a baby's pulse rate is more rapid than normal and will stabilize only by the end of the third month. His body temperature is also elevated at birth to reduce the shock of leaving the womb. A number of reflexes—automatic body responses—that help ensure his survival are also present. You can observe these reflexes operating in your own baby. There's a sneezing, a yawning, and a stretching reflex; there's the rooting reflex that causes the baby to turn and open his mouth to be fed when the side of his cheek is touched by his mother's breast or by the nipple on a feeding bottle; there's the startle reflex that makes the baby's arms and legs fly out wide and encircle anything within reach if

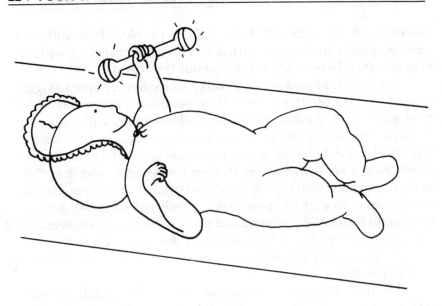

Visual Motor Development

he feels he is falling or if his crib has been suddenly jostled; there is the grasping reflex that causes his hand to close around something that is placed in his palm; and noticeable within about one week after birth is the visual avoidance reflex that causes a baby to close his eyes and try to get out of the way of anything that quickly approaches his face. But more important, there are other reflexes that slowly, over time, become modified and develop into the beginnings of intellectual activity.

At birth, the lower parts of the brain are in control of the baby's behavior. These control centers are similar to those that manage the entire repertory of behavior in lower animals, and they function mainly to ensure survival. The further development of the nervous system proceeds in a very organized and direct manner: from the head down to the base of the spine (cephalo-caudal development) and from the center of the body out to the toes and fingers (proximal distal development).

During the first couple of weeks, it is important for a baby to establish his own body as a solid object and begin to orient it to his physical space. One of the first areas in which this development can be seen is in the coordination between the information he receives from his eyes and the sensations that come from his body. When you lift your baby you will notice that his eyes and body begin to coordinate with each other. This doll-like eye movement (see page 188) indicates that vision and posture have begun to organize themselves in relationship to the pull of gravity on the baby's body, and the process will be well established sometime between the second and third weeks.

The rapidly developing visual system requires stimulation in the form of varieties of light and patterns of light in order for normal growth to continue. Numerous studies have shown that if the infant's retina is not stimulated by light, the visual system may actually stop in its development. Moreover, research with animals has shown that there must be pattern light stimulation as well. Special nerves called feature detectors will begin to lose their ability to respond to details in the absence of pattern stimulation—these nerves may atrophy, resulting in some forms of blindness.

If you watch your baby carefully, you can observe how he reacts to light stimulation with a hunger and satisfaction that is akin to that expressed when he has been fed. Notice how he is transfixed by shadows dancing on the wall, how he starts to look around selectively for things of interest. What attracts his attention most are things that provide pattern stimulation—not objects of just one color or tone, but objects of varied tones; and not just colored things, but objects with sharp differences in their details, such as swirls, checkerboard patterns, lines, grids, and the like. He appears to have a craving for this type of stimulation and is demonstrating for you the built-in need to provide his visual system with the thing necessary for its growth.

For most babies, their normal environment has enough pattern stimulation to elicit sufficient response from the feature detector nerves. In a study of children reared in hospital cribs, the mere placement of crib mobiles was shown to provide satisfactory stimulation. The study also showed that overwhelming children with too much stimulation can lead to a higher state of anxiety than is desirable for healthy growth. So don't overwhelm your baby with too many things to look at. A little at a time is preferable.

During the third month, a baby's visual system is almost prepared to retain all the information it receives. The sheath of fatty tissue, called myelin, that surrounds the nerves has extended to cover those nerves that enter the cerebral cortex. The myelin sheathing helps the nerves to send their messages to the brain but at birth this tissue covered only the baby's optic nerve and went as far back as the lower part of the brain. Now the nerves leading to the higher centers of the brain, the parts responsible for more intellectual judgments about what is being seen, begin to function. Brainwave signals that occur only when visual information is being actively studied are now detectable in the baby. During the first two months infants do not show this brainwave activity.

Visual examinations of babies up to the age of two and one-half months indicate that when their eyes are open and alert, they are most often focused at 8 inches. Here again, it appears that nature has had a hand in preparing the newborn child for important responses and adaptations to his environment, because 8 inches is just about the distance between a mother's eyes and a baby's eyes when she is holding the infant in her arms. Actually, before the third month, the baby's attention is not often directed at his mother's eyes, but rather at her mouth or the outside frame of her face. At three months, with the nerves to the cerebral cortex beginning to function, the baby starts to take an interest in the inside areas of her face, especially the eyes. Because of the tremendous importance of eye-to-eye contact between baby and mother in the social and emotional development of the child, let's look a little more closely at the processes that were at work during the first three months.

In the first week, visual information is responded to with a high degree of clarity within the nervous system. If a week-old baby looks at a very small object anywhere within his field of vision, we know that his nervous system responds even if he does not show any obvious reaction. The lower brain is apparently ready to respond to very small objects in the baby's environment, but the higher brain centers are not ready to allow a *perceptual* response. However, an object approximately one-quarter of an inch in size held 8 to 10 inches away from him will cause some small eye-tracking responses. This size, interestingly, is about the size of the cornea of the human eye, and it appears that the week-old baby's visual system is prepared to respond *behaviorally* to something that size only when it is 8 to 10 inches away, although the baby can see it at much greater distances. This demonstrates that at the earliest age the mechanisms for establishing eye-to-eye contact, which is necessary for the development of social relationships, are present and functioning.

The need for socialization is part of the built-in program that assures the survival of the baby. Socialization allows him to become part of a family, a social order, a community. Beginning in the first week after birth, a baby will display imitative behavior that is the start of social contact with other people. He will stick out his tongue, flutter his eyelids, and open and close his mouth in response to these actions by others. But these are reflex responses, triggered on an involuntary basis. By the second week he begins to smile at the sound of a human voice, but again this is a reflex smile rather than a social smile. Shortly after this his hearing is sufficiently developed to differentiate between sounds and to determine their location. He begins to organize the space around him through the sounds he hears and learns to turn his eyes in the direction of these sounds. He learns to recognize his mother's voice and will look at her mouth when she speaks. By the end of the first month, the mother's mouth becomes the center of the baby's attention.

During the second month a baby begins to signal the satisfaction that he gets from the relationship that is developing with his mother. If he is held so that his face is 8 to 10 inches from his mother's, he can focus on her eyes and return her smile. Very soon, by two and one-half months, he is returning a true social smile which expresses the love bond that has been established with her. Frequently you can see mothers playing with their babies by moving their heads toward their children and then away, into the 8 to 10 inch distance from the baby's eyes and then beyond it, while talking or singing to them. You are then witnessing a portion of nature's game plan: eye-to-eye contact, used to establish

Intimate Space Development

a bond that is a critical experience in the development of human beings. It is during this stage of development that a baby begins to discover his first perceptual space. In this space the baby can see little more than half of his mother's face. He can feel, smell, and taste her, but it is truly his intimate space because he integrates all these sensations as he focuses on her eyes.

Many investigators have measured how clearly infants and children can see. Usually these results are reported as a fraction, such as 20/20, which is a measure of visual acuity. This is, in reality, an adult way of examining a child's world. To get a clearer picture of what a child sees, I feel it is important to consider what a child's needs are. These needs are, mainly, to learn about his world and how to get along in it. For this, he needs support and, fortunately, his mother has been waiting all along to supply it. When a baby establishes eye contact with his mother and signals his appreciation of her presence by returning her smile, he has established that he can see her eyes clearly. After examining many infants and children over the past twenty years, as well as reading extensively in the literature on child development, I have come to the conclusion that when we measure an infant's acuity, we are really measuring the distance at which he can clearly see a human eye so as to maintain eye contact and signal to the other person that he wants to be involved with her. Acuity measurements are then really measures of the distance at which a baby is ready to socialize. An impression that I have formed from years of clinical experience, although not that well supported by laboratory research, is that the distance within which an infant can *maintain* a social relationship is defined by the distance at which he demonstrates completed binocular development—that is, two-eyed vision.

During the first three months after birth, a baby's social and emotional development is at an oral and passive stage. He is dependent on his primary caregiver, his mother, to provide food, comfort, and affection. He gains control from sucking and having his mouth full. This is an extremely important period in the baby's life because, as he becomes satisfied, he develops trust in the people around him and in his environment. If his needs are not met consistently, he will develop distrust. During this period a baby slowly starts to become an intellectual individual in his own right. But the first place that he must focus on is his own body.

In summary, the first three months are an important milestone in your child's life. The first month is spent organizing

Peripheral Awareness Development

himself so that the next two months can be directed to his very first important mission in life: establishing contact and rapport in his new world. All his energies are directed toward orienting his eyes, ears, mind, and emotions to focus on his primary caregiver. The three-month period culminates in your baby's having a body that is warm (temperature stabilized), balanced to gravity, and quiet (in the sense that his nervous system has become adapted to the new environment). He can orient his head, eyes, and ears to his mother, and maintain eye contact with her. He knows when she is talking, where the words come from, and can track her comings and goings with his eyes. If his needs are consistently satisfied, he begins to trust his new world. The special bond between baby and mother is strengthened each time they smile at each other, and the baby's smile is beholden to his visual system's ability to adjust its focus and hold its attention on his mother's eyes. This important relationship will determine your baby's ability to make vital human connections in the future.

Symptoms to Watch For by the End of the Third Month

If you notice any of these signs or symptoms, contact your pediatrician or behavioral optometrist right away.

1. Any mark on the face caused by delivery instruments.
2. Difficulty in opening each eyelid fully.
3. Mucus in either eye that makes the lids stick together.
4. Eyes that do not look clear and bright.
5. Difficulty your baby has in following you in all directions with his eyes.
6. Pupils that do not seem to respond to light.
7. Failure of your baby to respond to a sound by turning his eyes toward the sound.
8. One eye that does not seem to look at you and that appears to look constantly in one direction.
9. Failure to recognize food when it is brought.
10. Failure to try to maintain eye contact.

Things to Do in the First Three Months

1. If your baby does not move around in his crib much, make sure that you give him an opportunity to have an unobstructed view on both sides, so that he can use both eyes. If the crib is against one wall, change his position so that each eye has a chance to see out through the crib bars.
2. Make sure your baby has a chance to view patterns, especially changing patterns. Sometimes a light behind a moving mobile will cast some interesting shadows upon his wall for him to inspect.
3. Speak to your baby no matter where in the room you are.
4. When you are dressing or feeding your baby, make sure that he has a lot of opportunities to focus his eyes on your eyes. Remember that he can see your eyes clearly if you are approximately 8 to 10 inches away from his face.
5. Give him plenty of opportunities to follow you with his eyes, to his right, to his left, upward toward his head, and downward toward his toes.

The First Three Months

Motor Development

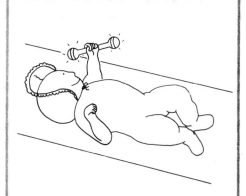

Visual Motor Development

Binocular Development

Peripheral Awareness Development

Intimate Space Development

Social Development

FOUR MONTHS TO EIGHT MONTHS

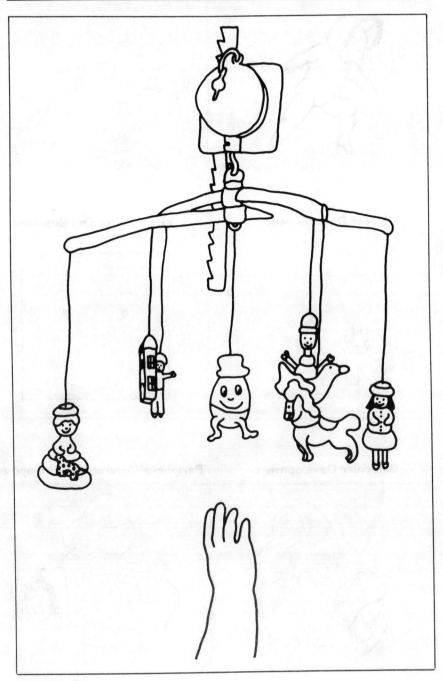

Reaching Out

The first three months represent the first platform on life's ladder. At this time your infant will have oriented himself to his new world and will have begun a relationship that will steer his course throughout life. During the next phase, which will last until about eight months of age, the attachment between mother and baby will grow stronger. This love and support will provide him with the confidence to explore new territory, using his newly developed perceptual skills to sort out what is important to him.

It is an interesting paradox that while your child is developing this deeper attachment and love, he is also preparing to separate himself and establish his own identity. During the period from four to eight months, your child's behavior is characterized by this preparation for separation.

The baby will now begin to view his mother more clearly as a separate object in space. The more he does this, the more anxious he will become when strangers approach, for by his reasoning, if his mother is a separate object in space, she could be taken away. At the end of this phase, he will smile less and less at strangers—quite different behavior than at the beginning, when he will smile at everyone who approaches to look at or play with him. Perhaps this stranger anxiety has evolved as a necessary protection for the vulnerable infant.

During this phase, your baby will begin to have a more stable pulse rate. Although his body temperature is basically normalized, he will still prefer to be bundled when he sleeps. His control over his body will continue to progress nicely—he already has gained control over his eyes, head, and neck; his head no longer lags behind his body when you pull him to a sitting position. About this time, he will no longer be confined to one side of his body when he is lying on his back in the crib, in a TNR position—a tonic neck reflex—like a fencing position with one arm out, the eyes, head, and upper trunk turned toward that arm, and often the leg as well. Now he will be on his back in an SNR position—a symmetrical neck reflex position, which allows him to survey the entire world in front of him. Most important, he is now becoming able to coordinate the movement of his upper body so that while lying on his back, he can survey everything that goes on in front of him. Now, when he wants to follow something visually, such as his mother as she walks across his field of view, he can track her the entire way without losing sight of her.

The lower body is also working hard to keep up in its development. Although he is not yet ready, he can show you signs of what is to come if you help him stand because he will be able, briefly, to support his weight by himself. This ability is a precursor to the start of his spatial independence.

At four months he will have learned to control his eye muscles sufficiently to be prepared to coordinate their use with movements of his trunk and arms in order to reach out. He will then begin to manipulate the things around him so as to understand and control them. This process is the beginning of "object permanence," of recognizing what objects are—the start of an inner language of concepts, such as hard, soft, round, and edged, that precedes his verbal language. It is an awareness of the different categories of objects, that some objects have sharp edges and others have smooth rounder edges, a beginning awareness of the differences between squares and circles. He also begins to become aware that some objects have no give. They are hard and can be trusted to support his weight while others are soft. When you push on them, they give in to the weight. In preparation for this development he will practice grasping, although his efforts may appear somewhat awkward. He will particularly have some difficulty in releasing objects, but by the time he has become able to reach out and grasp things with his fingers he will also be able to release them with more aplomb.

A great deal of physical development is going on at this time, and much of it is designed to prepare your baby for the great strides he will soon be taking toward mastering his environment. As adults, we are frequently advised to warm up before we enter into any physical activity. Apparently, your baby already knows this advice. You can see him exhibit this knowledge when he rolls from side to side, kicks his legs as if he were jogging, and flails his arms back and forth. All of these movements are preparatory to the physical activity in which he will soon be engaged.

Around the four-month period, the baby's nervous system is becoming more organized and complete. The primitive reflexes that he demonstrated before, in order to ensure survival, are no longer present or are beginning to fade. Some have slowly become harnessed under a growing intellect. He is reaching that point when his survival will be more dependent upon his own actions. He will roll over and sit alone for a period of time.

During this phase he will also begin to develop binocularity, the ability to use both eyes together. This ability makes it possible for him to guide his hands to the things he wants to grasp and

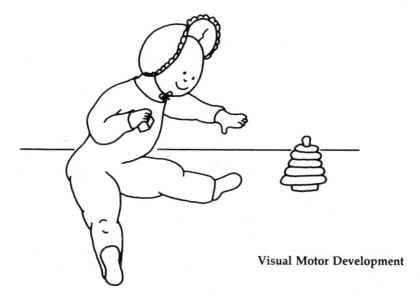

Visual Motor Development

examine, and facilitates his capacity to explore and know the quality and texture of objects in his world. It seems as if the visual system is programmed just now to develop the ability to judge space and to make possible the manipulation of objects in space, all in preparation for that time when he will begin to move out into the world.

So binocular development is the foundation for judging the location of things in space, and as your child develops this ability to coordinate his two eyes together he will be enticed to move out and explore his surroundings. First he will do this with his eyes guiding his hands, and then guiding his entire body. You will notice that his ability to track objects that move toward or away from him also improves now. This is a very important mechanism because it is the start of his acquiring judgment as to the distance objects are in relation to himself, and this is another way of learning that he is separate from the other things in his world. He is beginning to become an individual entity in space.

Up until four months, the protective covering of the nerves (myelin) had not completed its growth. In terms of vision this meant that what the baby perceived was more influenced by things going on in his environment than it was by his conscious control. Now, with increased brain activity, visual information is being analyzed by the baby. He is becoming capable of making decisions about how to categorize the events he observes and, ultimately, how to control them. He will begin to recognize objects that are social, and therefore merit a social smile, as opposed to those that are nonsocial and deserve more a look of curiosity.

Earlier, the mother received this social smile from her baby more often when she was within his intimate space, approximately 8 to 10 inches from his face. That was the distance at which he could most clearly see a human eye. Now you will notice that he smiles at her at a greater distance, the most frequent being around 2 feet. This has now become the distance at which he can most clearly see a human eye. As he looks at his mother's eyes, he can also take in almost all of her body, peripherally, which makes the 2-foot distance one that is most supportive of social contact. It allows for easy eye-to-eye contact, reciprocal smiling, and the use of body language to communicate. Soon, that form of communication will be taken over by a growing language ability, and the use of vision to communicate will be left to the language of intimacy, when one looks and sees love revealed in someone's eyes, or when an unspoken question is revealed just by eye contact.

As your baby gains more control over his eyes, you will notice that they work coordinately. Visual behavior at six months shows that eyes and head are linked together when a baby is surveying the environment. When your baby turns to look at something, he will also turn his head. Although he can more easily converge his eyes now, he will frequently lower his head and then raise it to help aim his eyes accurately when he is inspecting something. He will also widen his eyes by wrinkling or furrowing his brow when he wants to hold his visual attention on an object. These activities result because his neural development is not yet complete. While neural control has progressed nicely from his head down to his trunk, development frequently repeats itself, going over the same ground in order to prepare for a more complex level of behavior. In this case, the ability to examine the environment visually has not yet progressed to the point where eye movements are free from head and neck movements. This same linked coordination will occur again shortly before the age of three years. At that point, integrating body coordination for walking and visually scanning the environment will require that your child go back to moving his eyes and head in unison again, and it will remain that way until he has developed this more sophisticated control—walking and looking. After the integration occurs, he will be free to use his eyes and head separately but cooperatively.

This is another example of the spiral nature of development. It returns to places, events, and behaviors visited before, but now seen through new eyes with new insights.

By six months, it should be a rare occurrence for you to notice that your baby's eyes are not focused on the same object at the same time. If you do notice that one eye pays attention while the other does not, it is time for a developmental visual examination. Before this time, children will like looking at faces, even pictures of faces. But now that your baby uses both eyes together, a two-dimensional face is no longer interesting to him, for two eyes are for the purpose of gaining knowledge about where things are in space, a knowledge about depth, a three-dimensional view. Supporting this binocular ability, your baby will show a preference for real faces or three-dimensional masks, not for two-dimensional pictures.

At this point, objects are seen as solid and they are recognized for what they are, even if they are not fully in view. For example, an object that is partially hidden under a blanket will be under-

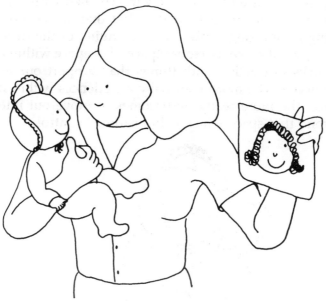

Social Development

stood as being a complete object, whereas before when something was partly hidden, your baby didn't recognize it at all. Also at this time, your baby has learned to coordinate his two hands and is beginning to use his thumb with his fingers. He can pull himself to a sitting or standing position and is just about ready to go out and act upon his world.

Right at this time, if we examined his eyes with a special light, we would notice that when he looks at an object close to him, he uses both eyes and analyzes what each eye tells him about that object. But this is only true in what we call the near space area—that space which is slightly beyond arm's length away. Another term for it is personal space. Perceptually, there are many spaces, each serving its own purpose.

At three months, the baby learned to focus on his mother's eyes and establish eye-to-eye contact, confirming that he was loved and supported. It enabled him to establish a deep emotional bond with her. The visual space in which that contact was made melded with his feeling, smelling, and touching space to form his intimate space—a space where very few people are allowed to enter—a space where little more than an eye is seen accompanied by other close, sensory information. At four months, because of the beginning development of space perception, your baby is able to look out into the world and locate things that are not part of himself, that are not intimately intertwined with his emotions—not part of his intimate space—but that are nevertheless interesting or amusing. This is the beginning of the development of his personal space. Personal space, that space within arm's reach, involves interaction with things that support our interests and our needs. The more your baby experiences within his personal space, the more ready he becomes to move out into the world beyond that space which is in his direct control.

Personal Space

Your baby has now reached the stage where he can coordinate his whole body; he can reach out with his eyes to see a thing that he would like to explore, his two eyes work together to determine the distance of that interesting object, and they allow him to guide his body toward it, grasp it, and examine it. Now you can see him extend his curiosity into yet another space where he will increase his explorations and examinations of the different objects that he sees. His interest will be extended to an area approximately 3 feet away from himself. Crawling marks the beginning of this phase. He is now ready to move out into his world. He has had adequate preparation—two eyes working together, two eyes judging where things are in space, an interest in the three-dimensionality of space, eyes guiding hands to explore objects in space, and a social sense that says, "Don't trust people you don't know out there." There are, however, two more things he must be able to do: he must know how to call his mother in case he's in trouble, and he must make sure that he does not smile at strangers.

Space is a new and not so orderly territory. It is a place that is away from the support and the attention of the baby's mother, although when he creeps out into that space, he will still be able to see and hear her. Nevertheless, he will still be more on his own and will be establishing his independence.

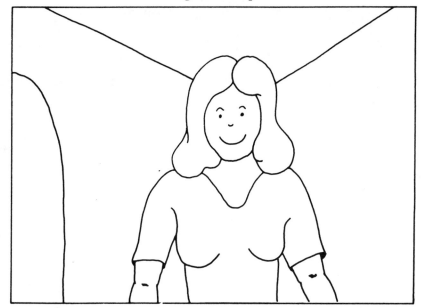

Peripheral Awareness

Signs of Development to Watch For
at Ages Four to Eight Months

1. Do both of your baby's eyes work together all the time? Or is there any appearance of strabismus—one eye looking at something while the other eye is looking somewhere else?
2. Does your baby pick up eye contact and show interest in the goings-on at a distance of two to three feet?
3. Does your baby spend time inspecting the objects in his environment? Does he inspect their position, texture, size, and so on? Does he show curiosity about things in the two- to three-foot distance?
4. Is your baby beginning to recognize objects that he has seen and has played with before? Can he recognize them if they are partially covered, when you ask him to find an object in an area near him?
5. Can your baby visually follow people and events across his entire visual field?
6. Do his face and eyes light up when he recognizes an object?

Things to Do for
Your Four- to Eight-Month-Old

1. Allow your baby time every day on his stomach with his field of view unobstructed so that he can watch the comings and goings of things in his field. Make sure there are interesting things to see at the 2- to 3-foot distance.
2. While he is lying on his back, provide an eye–hand gym for him to reach out and explore. It should have objects he can pull and objects he can control. Each day, place it so he can explore it with his feet as well as with his hands.
3. Provide your baby with objects of different textures, sizes, and weights to explore.
4. Occasionally place an object so that it is partially hidden by a blanket or by another object.
5. Label by verbally naming each object that he plays with and ask him to find it by calling it by its name.
6. Allow him to experience crawling under objects as well as climbing over them.

Four Months to Eight Months

Motor Development

Visual Motor Development

Binocular Development

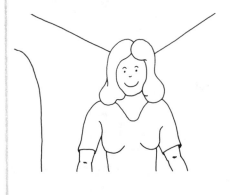

Peripheral Awareness Development

Personal Space Development

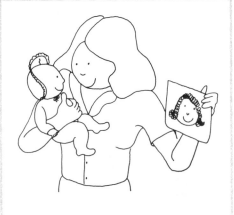

Social Development

NINE MONTHS TO EIGHTEEN MONTHS

Exploring Space

The first two phases of development—from birth to three months and from four to eight months—have prepared the ground for your baby to determine his own destiny. You will now find him moving out and trying to conquer his new world. Moving out and becoming independent require that he has fulfilled his prior needs satisfactorily so that he trusts that he will be able to handle himself. This is true up to a point. He is now able to hold an image of his mother in his mind so that he is free to travel to other rooms and places even though she is out of sight. But as time diminishes that image, he comes back to take another look, to fuel up and brighten the image, before he crawls off again. Sometimes he'll listen to his mother's activity, but more often these auditory messages will not be sufficient to sustain him, so he must come back and refresh his visual image of her.

This whole stage is a struggle to move out in many ways, to explore boundaries, and you will see a similar stage occur again when he is age four. The freedom to explore necessitates that your baby continue to develop his visual-motor skills and this leads to an increasing trend, from age nine months to sixteen months, to move into deeper territory. As your baby does this, he slowly begins to develop an understanding of his relationship to his environment.

Physical development moves apace. At this point he will begin to demonstrate his ability to release the things he holds onto with less difficulty. Soon this capacity to let go enables him to lower himself from a standing position, and this newfound freedom extends to the ability to counterbalance the left side of his body with the right side, forward movement with backward movement. Out of this emerges his ability to finally stand alone. If you watch carefully, you can observe how his visual system has aided this emerging ability by attending to the verticals of space so that when he stands alone, he can use his eyes to orient his body to vertical objects. But it is still a fragile accomplishment, for he will lose his ability to stand easily when he closes his eyes or when some important vertical object that he is attending to falls over. As soon as his means of vertical visual orientation alters, his motor vertical orientation goes down with it.

The integration that has developed between holding and releasing, which has permitted him to stand alone, must become a part of his movement repertory in order for him to walk alone. You can see this beautifully, but painfully, demonstrated as he struggles to walk and has to mediate propulsion and poise. Watch how he staggers forward and then stops and rocks. Notice how his upper torso will alternate between leading and resisting the needed counterthrusting of his two sides. At times the upper torso moves forward with the right leg; at times it holds back in the counterpoise necessary for graceful balance. It is almost as if you were witnessing the gait of animals in various stages of evolution, sometimes reptilian in nature and other times more mammalian. If you've ever driven a manual shift car, you can empathize with what your baby is going through. Remember the difficulty you had in coordinating the use of the clutch and accelerator? Until you learned, you drove the car the way your baby walks, in stops and convulsive starts.

At nine months, the baby is climbing up every piece of furniture, holding on so that he can stand up. As he approaches the end of his first year, he no longer tolerates lying still on his back, except when he's asleep. He becomes a powerhouse of energy, constantly looking into things, poking, prodding. His thumb and index finger begin a delicate partnership that will be very useful to him for the rest of his life—he begins to use them more to probe and pluck at things. He puts objects into other objects. He's now learning about the texture of the three-dimensional world. All of these explorations are actively guided and absorbed by his eyes. His developed eye-hand coordination permits him to bring objects to his mouth, and how better to know an object than to put it in your mouth! His eyes are now acting more like organs for dealing with sensory knowledge. All of the actions and reactions relating to textures are being keenly observed, recorded, analyzed, and stored away for future reference. At a later time, he'll be able to conjure up those images and recall what they look like, feel like, taste like, and what uses they have, just by looking into his mind's eye.

Notice how the storage of this information is being categorized. He is aware not only of the container, but also of the process of containing. Now he looks at the bottoms of all things that have tops. The formation of this way of looking at the world is the start of developing a sense of cause and effect, which will lead shortly to an increase in his ability to organize his impressions about the world so that he can move more freely in it. At first he will do this visually and physically, later mentally, and ultimately he will repeat the same learning socially and emotionally. This is the underlying pattern of development.

At ten months your baby has a fairly good ability to grasp objects, but he is not yet able to release them accurately. If you play a game of building a tower, he will be able to release a block in the near vicinity of another, but he does not have the accuracy to place it on top of another block. It is not that he doesn't see where to put the block; it's just that release functions usually develop somewhat later than grasp functions. The baby tends to be able to get involved before he can get disengaged. It will take until the fourteenth month before he demonstrates that he can release a block with precision so as to be able to pile three blocks, one on top of another.

The same sequence of development will occur with drawing. Scribbles and circles will be easier than crosses and squares because crosses and squares require a release from the movement, a stop, a change of position, and then a new movement to form the rest of the pattern. They require stopping ability and then reorientation. Of course, he will not start this kind of drawing until he's three-and-one-half years old and won't be able to get the pattern completely right until he's five. But you can get an insight into the kind of problem he's working to overcome when you watch him now trying to pile up blocks. Until release abilities are integrated with grasp functions, you will find that your child has difficulty with all forms of transition.

Visual Motor Development

The ability to perceive three-dimensionally that began for your child at about six months of age, with the ability to keep both eyes aimed where he wanted, enabled him to understand and store information about the solidness and permanence of objects and of people. As the months went on, he realized that a toy could be seen from many different positions and used in many different ways and still be the same toy. Before this time, the toy existed only in his mind, connected with what he did with it. Now the toy seems to him to have a life of its own, and it is always the same toy, even if it is partially hidden. For your baby, this is a big step forward in understanding the reality of the world. It is also a crucial step in developing imagery and using that imagery for language.

You can see the beginning of the development of imagery somewhere around the twelfth month when your baby begins purposely to imitate you or other people. Notice how he imitates your blinking or facial expressions. A similar sort of behavior might have occurred almost immediately after birth, but then it was a reflexive action. Now he does it for a purpose. Watch how he imitates the banging of blocks that he saw another child do the day before. This type of imitation is important because it shows he is beginning to use an image, a memory, of what he saw earlier.

The visual examination of your baby at twelve months will show that near space is well organized visually—both eyes focus coordinately, and accurately probe details. Midspace, the area from 3 to 10 feet, is just beginning to draw his attention and interest. The examination will also show that your baby can see a human eye clearly between 2 and 4 feet. This is the distance at which you will find it easiest to establish eye contact, and it is the distance at which your baby will frequently initiate social contact. When he looks at his mother's eyes, he will peripherally be able to see one or two other people standing next to her. Note

Binocular Development

how he now shifts attention from one person's eyes to the next. He is becoming aware that there are other people in his world with whom he can interact.

During the stage of moving up and out into the world, several things are being symbolically connected. Each time your baby

Social Development

Peripheral Awareness

moves away from you and then comes back for comfort and re-assurance, he becomes aware of the distance he can travel independently. This feeds his growing sense of autonomy. It also teaches him not to be afraid to explore his new skills. At this time, his father becomes an important figure in his life. Fathers are often more physical in their play than mothers, and they reward physical mastery and independence more often. This period of time is for forging ahead, expanding horizons, and using imagery to a greater extent to solve problems in the mind's eye, as well as sustaining his increasing distance from his mother.

It is important that your child be allowed to explore, always knowing and feeling support for his new growth. Unfortunately, some parents are not able to allow their children the physical and psychological space to explore. Some are, in fact, fulfilled by the close relationship of the earlier months and are not able to let go. The child squirms to be free but the parents hold on, preventing the freedom to move. If such a situation persists, it can create frustration and communicate fear, which inhibit the growth of exploration and independence.

I will never forget working with a patient who was not able to use his two eyes together. He could use only one eye at a time. My patient, an adult in his early thirties, had undergone many years of psychotherapy and at that time had had approximately one year of vision therapy. We had frequently gotten to the point where he could keep both of his eyes together on an object, but each time we were ready to break through and move to the next level of skills, he would regress. It was as if a little voice inside him were saying that to go beyond this point was not acceptable. He had worked on the same point in his psychotherapy, but to no avail. One day, we decided to work on coordinating both sides of his body, and he tried practicing a little creeping. No sooner had he begun to creep than he had a flash of insight. He recalled a scene from childhood in which he was playing with his father. He had just learned to creep, and as he would move away from his father, his father would grab him and hold him. He told me that it felt like he was being told not to experiment with coordinating the two sides of his body to creep away to freedom. As this insight was worked through in his psychotherapy, we were finally able, in his vision program, to develop full binocular vision.

As I look back over many years as a vision therapist, I recall many situations and events that can interfere with the development of an integrated visual system. One can inherit a damaged eye muscle or neural circuit, but I believe this is relatively rare. One can have a serious illness that interrupts the higher neural circuits at a critical phase of development. Examples of these kinds of situations are high fevers and the usual childhood illnesses, such as measles and mumps. The development of binocular vision can also be interfered with by emotional trauma, such as the loss of a loved one. However, a possible source of trouble that I have not yet seen addressed in the ophthalmic literature is the issue of what is accepted behavior for a baby and, therefore, rewarded and allowed to become a habit, as opposed to behavior that is not permitted and therefore falls into relative disuse or is actively, subconsciously blocked. The patient I mentioned above was given an unconscious message that the coordination of his body to explore and to become independent was not acceptable. If this message was reinforced at other times and in other ways, then it's no wonder that it became, symbolically, an obstacle each time he tried to integrate the two sides of himself.

Although between twelve months and three years the child is actively seeking to explore new territory, he is also ambivalent about exercising this new impulse. This is one of the reasons we frequently see wariness with strangers until approximately age three. Apparently, there is a built-in protective social mechanism. It is also why we see the need for a warm, soft security blanket. This acts as a substitute for a warm, soft, supportive mother. As your child achieves a greater distance from you, he will still need you, even if only symbolically. You will see this need for a security blanket increase in new and strange places, as well as in stressful situations.

Signs of Development to Watch For at Ages Nine to Eighteen Months

1. Is your baby interested in exploring his environment?
2. Is he able to move outside of eyesight of you while he explores?
3. Is he interested in exploring objects? Does he appear to note their size and shape? Does he explore depths, the inside of containers, boxes, jars, etc?

4. Does he visually judge the size of his body so that he doesn't continually bump his head as he crawls under things? Does he judge his width so that he is not continually frustrated by not fitting into too small a space?
5. Do his eyes guide his hands as he places marks on paper?
6. Can he pick up an object he wants and place it where he wants, like raisins in a cup or one block on another?
7. Does he recognize what objects are used for, like containers that can be used to scoop up water or sand?
8. Do events and people 2 to 4 feet from him attract and hold his attention?
9. Has he begun to play alongside other children, watching and sometimes imitating their play?

Things to Do for
Your Nine- to Eighteen-Month-Old

1. Give your baby the opportunity to look for his favorite toy in another room.
2. Give your baby opportunities to crawl under and over objects. Vary the size of the spaces.
3. Give your baby objects that he can push or pull. Pushing a ball or a box cannot only be great fun, it helps him learn to coordinate his body and control objects.
4. Provide objects that have to be carefully placed in a container, such as beads or buttons in a box. *Because these objects are small and can be swallowed, this activity has to be carefully supervised.*
5. Provide opportunities to stack objects such as pillows, blocks, etc.
6. Provide opportunities to judge distances. You can use a small stick with a magnet attached to it. Teach your baby how to fish for objects with the magnet.
7. Provide fat crayons and paper to scribble on.
8. Provide opportunities to play alongside another child his age. A good distance for the other child to be at is between 2 and 4 feet.

Nine Months to Eighteen Months

Motor Development

Visual Motor Development

Binocular Development

Peripheral Awareness Development

Intellectual Space Development

Social Development

2
The Toddler:
Eighteen Months
to Three Years

Parallel Play

Vision development is so important for your child that he started to practice using his eyes before birth. Immediately after birth, he could move his eyes with a fair degree of control, and shortly after that you found your baby practicing coordination between his hearing and his eye movements. The coordination between eye, ear, and posture provided him with the means to pay attention, to survive, and to learn. A crucial phase in vision development occurred at approximately three months when your baby learned to focus on his mother's eyes and exchange smiles. This established a warm bond and an enduring relationship. For your baby it also established a very personal space, called intimate space, integrating vision, touch, smell, and taste, inside a distance of about 8 inches from his body.

Shortly after this, your baby began to use his two eyes together, and by six months this skill provided him with the ability to grasp objects and bring them to his body. This led to his ability to bring objects into the space where he could study their textures and to confirm some of these visual discriminations by putting the objects into his mouth. Thus, you began to see the evolution of his personal space—the space that extends out to the end of his fingertips, approximately 10 to 12 inches.

It was at this time that he began to recognize that he is a separate entity in space and to develop spatial perception, with himself at one pole and external objects at the other. The process of categorizing the world of objects ensued, and as the months went on, he began to catalogue the various sensory qualities that objects reveal of themselves. As his eye-body coordination progressed, he demonstrated that he was able to integrate not only his eyes and his head, and eyes and hands, but gradually his eyes and trunk as well. This led to the next phase, in which visual-motor skills allowed him to move out into his surroundings. In this case, his eyes continued as active seekers of stimulation. Once they became attracted to something out of arm's reach, they compulsively propelled his body to seek it, all the while actively guiding his body through space. The need was to bring the object into his personal space area so he could visually and kinesthetically examine it. This whole sequence of events led to the development of intellectual space—that which extends out to approximately 20 inches. (It is interesting to conjecture on the relationship between that space and the fact that the average person who becomes nearsighted winds up with a focal point—the place of clearest vision—somewhere in this intellectual space area, that is, a focal point between 20 and 10 inches.)

As your child approaches his second birthday you will, I hope, have childproofed the doors and drawers and other areas that you do not want him to explore, for this little perpetual-motion machine will appear to be everywhere at once. His body appears to be constantly moving and turning—he has reached the stage where turning seems to be imposed upon him from within. Have you noticed that he likes to spin around until he falls down? He also likes to watch the turning motion of wheels and records, and will explore the turning motion of bottle caps and door knobs. He also really enjoys making round scribbles on paper.

At this time, he will be able to move his eyes from one object to another with greater facility and with less extraneous body movement. Looking out into space no longer requires that he move out to where he is looking as he did when he was eighteen months old. He now knows more about where things are in space, and he can look out and maintain contact with others without having to move his body into that space. Although his eyes move smoothly and can do so without a corresponding movement of his head, his eyes and hands are not yet independent of trunk movement. You can see this when he reaches out for something and has to twist his trunk in order to get it. This sometimes gets him into trouble, as when he walks or runs and tries to pick something up, especially if that object is moving too. In reaching, he will frequently find that his body is in the wrong orientation to make contact with the object. However, his eye-body coordination will have progressed so that he can walk and turn his eyes and head without having to reorient his body and take himself in a different direction.

He can walk without regarding other objects, such as curbs and steps, and now is able to walk up and down steps alone because he does not have to actively, visually guide his body. He can pay attention, peripherally, to where his body is going. During this stage, spatial words begin to take on a new importance. Although he uses words like *where* and *there*, he does not yet have the concept of the space between *here* and *there*. He begins to develop this concept by repeatedly asking questions about where he is going and how he will get there.

At approximately age two, his personal space area is well developed. We now see him pay more attention to integrating his growing language ability with his visual ability. Together these two, vision and language, will form the foundation upon which academic learning will prosper or flounder, so you will see your child now increasingly interested in pictures. He will be labeling and identifying the pictures and the things shown in them. He

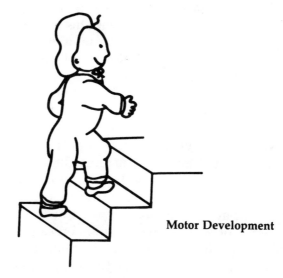

Motor Development

increasingly uses spatial words such as *where* and *there,* and will more often use words to guide his actions. It now becomes more important than ever to help your child explore the different qualities of objects. Encourage him to focus on what things are and what they do, as well as what they are not and cannot do. In this way, you will help him begin to see the inclusive and exclusive properties of things and also the labels that are attached to objects and events.

Visual Motor Development

The new, increased freedom he has between eye and hand shows up while he is playing with his toys. Previously, he needed his eyes to guide his hands in order to maintain his attention and skillfully play with a toy. Now, with his growing visual-motor ability, he can visualize what his hands should do, and he is free from having to continuously look at what he is doing. This is, of course, only true when he plays with his toys and other objects that he knows very well. Nevertheless, the freedom he obtains in vision and movement allows him to look ahead. As a result, he is beginning to show some foresight. He will be experimenting less and less on a physical level now and increasingly on an internal, mental level. This is the precursor of the shift to the imagery or imagination stage. Just watch him when he comes to a closed door with his hands full. You can almost see the wheels turning as he looks at the door and then at his full hands. Shortly, he will put down his toys or whatever he is holding and approach the door to open it. Just as he is about to reach for the doorknob he stops, looks back and forth from door to toys again, then goes back and pushes the toys out of the way. He has imagined what the door will look like when it is opened and noted that it would open on his toys. Satisfied that he has moved his things far enough away so he can open the door, he goes to it and opens it, retrieves his toys, and walks through. Don't expect him to close the door after himself; that has to wait until he develops an understanding of what is right and wrong or what behavior is expected of him, which will occur somewhere around the age of three. What you see now is his ability to look ahead and think of the solution to a problem. There are times when the newfound skill is just on the boundary of his ability. Then you may see some image-regressive behavior, as he imagines what to do and simultaneously tries it out with his body: he opens and closes his mouth as he tries to figure out how to open a locked drawer, or his hands imitate a pair of scissors as he figures out how he is going to cut something.

And so he has developed fairly good visual-motor skills. His eyes now coordinate his entire body as he moves through space. He will have to refine these skills in the next couple of years, but he now demonstrates greater freedom between his eyes and his head. His binocular coordination has progressed so that his two eyes share information in the near spatial areas, out to approximately 30 inches. Although he demonstrates an awareness of depth, so that it is unlikely that he will knowingly propel himself off a step, finer three-dimensional vision is not yet part of his repertory. His eyes and hands now work together so well that they have formed an intimate partnership. One does not need constantly to check the other. His movements are no longer guided by active looking, but by a visual memory of the necessary motor plan. Visual memory is used to plan and guide his movements. This frees your child to actively look ahead while he is engaged in an activity, and this, in turn, allows for the development of further visual memory, imagination, role-playing, and foresight. At the same time, another important development is occurring, and that is his growing command of language.

During this next phase, you will see the continuing growth of his visual-memory skills and further integration of visual-language skills. In both of these areas, your child's vision plays a very important role. Also significant is the role vision plays in his social growth, for now his visual acuity has progressed so that he can see a person's eye from between 5 and 8 feet. Eye-to-eye

Binocular Development

contact, which started his whole intercourse with life, is the enticement that causes him now to pay attention to the world outside of his hands, and so you will see him extend his interests into this midspace area.

At about this time, his interests begin to change with regard to other people as well. While his mother is still the most important person in his life, he now wants to begin interacting with other people—he is moving out into conversational space, his social-visual space. Social contact is most easily obtained for him at the distance of between 5 and 8 feet, the distance he can best see a human eye. If his eye-teaming skills are developing properly, they will now help to support his ability to visually concentrate on the tasks in which he's involved.

Unfortunately, this is an age when binocular development too frequently becomes disrupted. It is not unusual for parents to report that they occasionally notice one eye drifting toward the child's nose. Over the years, I have noticed that children who have interrupted binocular development have difficulty in main-

Social Development

taining visual concentration, as well as in maintaining social contact. If binocular development is proceeding properly, then your child can not only see another person's eyes at 5 to 8 feet, but he can also peripherally see three or four other people at the same time, which seems to be a preparation for group play. If your child does not show an interest in continuing play with his peers, look more closely at his eye-teaming skills. The usual age for developing these social behaviors is between two and three years.

This is the age when you will begin to see your child's mental

Peripheral Awareness

imagery used more and more to help establish his role vis-à-vis other family members and playmates. His imaginary play allows him to practice everyday social skills, and it is a key to his continued visual-motor development. You will now see him pretending to go shopping or bringing the car to the garage to be fixed. His mother may one day be shocked to find her closet a mess and her makeup kit missing, but the cause of this event will be quite clear when she goes to the playroom and finds her child all decked out for a night at the Ritz. What she is witnessing is a fertile mind in operation, imagining objects and actions in new relationships. He is learning to infer and draw conclusions, to move his mind out into space and practice what it is like to be in a new environment. He is examining the limits and boundaries of social interaction as he did before in exploring the limits and actions of physical objects. In doing this, he is learning the established rules of a social order in the same way he learned the rules governing physical objects. You will also see him practicing influencing others when he is at play with other children. In these situations, the children sit at play, each apparently doing his or her own thing, but being subtly influenced by the play of the others. They communicate and influence each other indirectly, by imitating and being imitated. At a later time, they will influence each other less through their physical actions and more through their language.

Social Space

This is an important time for fathers. The father's role in the child's development is becoming more pronounced, for he serves as a role model when dealing with unpredictable situations. A child's play with his father frequently tends to be more unpredictable and physically stimulating. Fathers often encourage attempting new things that don't always work out the way the child expects them to. They encourage tackling problems with confidence and their play is often creative and vigorous, pushing the child to search the boundaries of his imagination.

You must have considerable patience now because although at one moment your child may show an ability to focus on small details intensely, he is also in an oppositional stage, so that he will have difficulty in integrating his needs and his wants, his attention with his distractability. He wants help, yet he dislikes intrusion into his personal, mental world. He has a drive to enrich his intellectual development visually, tactually, and verbally, and yet he feels pulled to get up and explore the outer territories, the space of new places and new faces. By the time he reaches two and a half years, his visual skills in the near visual area, within arm's reach, will be fully integrated and binocular. He will continue to explore, visually, the contours and depths of objects and the nuances of those objects. His visual-motor skills will have progressed to the point where he begins to draw things and you will note that your child has developed the orientation for drawing vertical and horizontal lines. He will also be focusing on the qualities of things and the categories in which they belong.

During this difficult time for the parents, there will be frequent accidents (stumbling and bumping into things), stuttering, stammering, and the tendency for an eye to drift. If you notice that your child has difficulty in coordinating his eyes, arrange immediately for him to be seen by a developmental optometrist. Although it is only a phase, it is a good time to do something about it to ward off the possibility of its becoming a permanent fact of life.

Signs of Development to Watch For at Ages Eighteen Months to Three Years

1. Is your baby able to walk around familiar territory without having to constantly watch what he is doing? Curbs, steps. . . .
2. Is he interested and skillful in playing with puzzles, pieces, and toys such as Legos?
3. Is he beginning to use and understand spatial words like under, over, there?
4. Can he find a hidden object by following a simple set of spatial directions?
5. Does he demonstrate that he is beginning to think over his actions beforehand?
6. Does he demonstrate a growing understanding of words that define the qualities of objects, e.g. soft, smooth, hard, etc?
7. Is he beginning to play cooperatively with another child?
8. Is his play imaginative?
9. Does he show an interest in people and events out to 8 feet?

Things to Do for Your Eighteen-Month- to Three-Year-Old

1. This is the time to start a simple gymnastics program that gets more sophisticated as your child grows.
   Start with sets of large pillows and cardboard boxes that are used as steps. Make mountains to climb and slides to roll down.

As your child grows, change to equipment that requires more skillful use of his body in all positions; stepping, sliding, twisting, turning, bending, etc.

Make sure that you make a bridge to walk across. As his balance improves, make the bridge narrower.

2. Play games involving running and kicking a beach ball to his partner.
3. Play catch and batter-up with a balloon.
4. Make a maze that he has to navigate with his wagon.
5. Provide play dough or clay. At times, let his imagination run free; at other times, suggest a design. (All products should be honestly praised.)
6. Give your child beads to string. Let him make his own design as well as follow one you have made.
7. Provide him with puzzles. At first large wooden puzzles with 3 pieces and, as his skill increases, give him puzzles with more pieces that are smaller.
8. Let him cut out pictures to make his own book of familiar people and objects.
9. Provide him with a set of large Legos or a set of large wooden screws and nuts.
10. Read books together and have him point out the differences between objects; big/small, open/closed, thin/fat, dog/cat, etc.
11. Give him crayons and plenty of paper to draw upon. A large easel would be nice.
12. Provide objects and clothing to stimulate dress-up imagination games. Let him deliver the mail to people in the family.

Eighteen Months to Three Years

Motor Development

Visual Motor Development

Binocular Development

Peripheral Awareness Development

Social Development

3
The Preschooler:
Ages Three and Four

THE THREE-YEAR-OLD

Meet My Friends

A three-year-old is a social animal. His interests are in people and places. You can talk to him; at times you can even reason with him and bargain with him.

He has come a long way from the time when he first learned to roll over. Now he can jump high and far. Not only is he able to coordinate his movement with feet planted on the ground, but he is now able to move coordinately, and, as a result, he delights in climbing jungle gyms, in galloping, and, by age four, even in beginning to roller skate. The implication is that there is a more adultlike organization of neural control over the entire body, the top and bottom integratively. You can notice this as you watch him walk, arms swinging like a miniature adult. He even begins to alternate his feet when going up the stairs. By age four he will begin to alternate his feet going down the steps.

This same neuromotor coordination of opposite sides shows up in the control of the eyes. A child's eyes work together as a team now, especially in the personal-space area through to the intermediate or social-space area. This two-eye teaming allows him to more accurately locate where things are in his spatial environment. The increased interaction between the right and left

Motor Development

eyes allows him to attend more to what he is looking at and therefore become more involved in that space and the people who occupy it. Before, he was more interested in attending to what he was doing. What interests him now is the space of social group interaction, somewhere between 7 and 10 feet. It is a space that he was showing interest in when he was two and a half, and now that his binocular skills are more complete, it is a space that he is freer to interact in.

Two other developments help him to occupy this spatial area. The first is the continuing freedom he has from actively, visually guiding his actions. His visual-motor skills have progressed, as we noted at age two and a half, to the point where he could direct his movements through a visual image of the required action. This freed him to develop foresight and plan ahead. He is no longer situation-bound. Planning ahead allows for more imaginative play, which increases at this age. He could be the garbage man or a firefighter, or he and his friend could hide in the castle as the monsters pound at the door downstairs. The level of visual-motor integration he now has also allows the three-year-old to be more aware of his movements in space so that he is more able to predict those movements. As a result we see him participate more readily in games of catch. At first, his reach is more of a whole arm thrust in order to interrupt the ball's path. Later, there is more coordination of hands reaching out for the ball.

The second development that helps to orient him more in this area of social space is his growing use of language. Although the increase in vocabulary allows him to label more things, it is also the interaction of verbalizing with visually focusing that helps him to develop these skills. He now more readily focuses on a facial expression and on body language to see and determine the effects of his words and he will at times adjust his words and actions accordingly. We also see this growing interaction between vision and language as we examine him when he looks at a book and searches for the words to describe what he sees. As he searches for a word, you can see his whole body freeze until the right word is found, and then the tension is released. The same intensity of focus is noted on examining his eyes as he searches for the meaning of a word. As soon as the meaning is found, the intense focusing is released. At this age the search for meaning or labeling is being integrated with the search for the previously filed image of that experience. There is an intensity to the visual search until a match is found between the image and the word. At a later age, when we examine good readers, we find that this search is so fluid that it passes too quickly for an examiner to measure it.

Focusing, which started at three months as a means to maintain eye contact and socialize with a love object (the mother), has slowly been modified so that it is the means for establishing social rapport and for judging, by focusing on the other person's expressions, whether that person understands and wants to maintain that rapport. We can call this the minor theme of focusing. The major theme is the use of focusing to determine the qualities of objects in the environment and then to associate these images of qualities with the growing language skills. And so the child increasingly uses words to describe previous experiences of space— *back, over, under,* and so on—as well as experiences of the size, color, number, and dimensions of objects.

As your child's visual-motor skills developed, he was free to plan and to predict movement through space, and so he began to develop more of a time sense. We begin to see this now in his understanding of time and space and in the words and phrases he uses, such as "all the time" or "for the past two weeks." He understands different times of the year. He understands that he is required to do different things at different times. This is one of the reasons that you can begin to bargain with him, for he now understands what it means when you say, "I'll do it in a little while, honey."

His newfound visual-motor integration allows him to orient to a situation more easily and more quickly. Now you will notice that his drawings are confined to the paper and do not overlap onto the kitchen table. Also, when he enters a familiar room with familiar things, his ability to orient himself and involve himself productively shows a startling difference from just one year ago. In a study done at the Gesell Institute for Child Development, children's meanderings in a nursery school room were monitored for seven minutes. The two-year-olds, who were given seven items scattered around the room to play with, were observed bounding back and forth between five of the available items. They spent more time moving from one toy to another, from one situation to another, than they did playing with any toy or in any situation. However, with the three-year-olds there was a very large difference. They immediately, upon observing the scene, selected the toys or situations they wanted to be involved with. They tended to make some movements in and around the area of the toy and then change their minds and run off to play with another toy. In other words, there was more involvement for a purpose than there was movement for movement's sake.

The ability to freely shift the eyes without having to shift the body, and the ability to mentally monitor his actions, has allowed the three-year-old to develop an overall picture of his involvement and a plan to start and finish that involvement with his tasks. We see this in his selection of toys to play with, the places to play in, the people to interact with, and the pictures to copy. This sense of order allows him to orient himself easily to a situation so that he is freer to plan a little in advance. His ease in orientation allows him the freedom to take in new interests in his visual environment. He recognizes landmarks when he goes to new places, and he anticipates them on his return trips. They satisfy his growing sense of order. He is more interested in completing things; in fact, he is troubled by parts that are missing from toys or by furniture that is not in the right place. Because he doesn't

Visual Motor Development

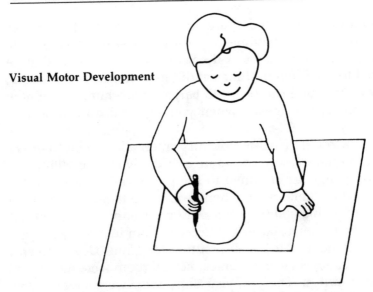

swing from one thing to another, he is calmer and more satisfied and therefore less negative. He is a joy and a relief to a mother harried by a previously out-of-sorts two-and-one-half-year-old. Generally, the three-year-old is in better harmony with himself and his environment. It is as if the sun came out after a summer squall.

The child now is able to shift his attention and focus from near to far, from outside to inside, from the general to the specific, with much greater ease. It is another sign of his growing integration. Although the three-year-old uses his two eyes together, he is not yet fully binocular. Visual examinations still show periods of one-eye usage. Because the neuropsychological binocular circuits have not yet been fully integrated, he is vulnerable to losing this still newly acquired skill. He can lose it if he is ill, if he runs a high fever, or if he contracts one of the usual childhood illnesses such as measles or chicken pox. This is also true if he experiences a personal or emotional trauma, like the loss of a loved one or abandonment by one or both parents. I have seen patients in clinical practice who developed a strabismus after they were abandoned to the care of social agencies or distant relatives. In cases such as these, attempting to correct the ocular situation by itself is not always successful. Frequently coordination between the visual therapist and a psychotherapist is necessary. This is also true of those patients who have sought relief through psychotherapy alone. Although the emotional trauma precipitated the visual problem, working with feelings and insight is insufficient to resolve the visual problem. The patient must learn how to use his eyes, to trust what he feels when he looks, and also to understand his feelings.

The three-year-old phase of development is relatively quiet and secure; however, it is frequently short and precedes another short period of instability, at age three and a half, when your child is likely to be prone to breakdowns in his binocular skills. Because of this, three is a good age for a visual examination, to try to ensure that the turmoil of the next phase of disequilibrium at age three and a half can be weathered. Three and a half represents a transitional age before the greater integration and expansiveness of four arrives. At three and a half, it is not unusual to see similar unsteadiness, confusion, poor eye-hand coordination, and loss of binocular skills as was seen at age two and a half. What your child wants to do is not in phase with his coordination skills. He sees new relationships and jumps ahead of himself before he has a clear picture of how to go from one thing to another. He may try to build a pyramid of three blocks upside down with the single block on the bottom. Although he sees two of the blocks on the bottom and the single one on top, he may focus on the last block in the sequence of perceived movements, the single one. This, then, is the first one he moves, and he therefore winds up trying to make the pyramid upside down. Because his ability to organize the total experience is so fragile at this age, he may not allow anyone to talk to him when he is working or even to move into his peripheral field, as it tends to lead his planned sequence in other directions. The tenuousness of his coordination is pervasive. We see it in poor eye-hand coordination, frequent blinking, stuttering, difficulty with heights, and in sudden onset of strabismus.

During this period there is a tendency for the child to exaggerate his egocentricity. When he bumps into a chair, he complains that the chair hit him: "Naughty chair!" He believes in the consciousness of inanimate objects. (Not until the age of seven do children believe that conscious life is only reserved for animals and people.) At age three and a half, there is an exaggeration of illogical, intuitive, and magical thinking. It is no wonder that children who develop visual problems at this age later show an increase of this kind of regressive thinking. It is not until their perceptions are sorted out that we can expect their observations will yield more logical and realistic results.

As your child approaches his fourth birthday he will demonstrate ease in having eye contact between 10 and 16 feet. This

Peripheral Awareness

is the distance at which he can clearly see a human eye. As he holds eye contact, he will be able to monitor peripherally what amounts to a small classroom. You will also notice that he can maintain concentrated visual attention at this distance. He now demonstrates that he is ready for sustained group activities and perhaps a good nursery school experience. At four years of age his mental activity will more and more replace physical activities by the use of images and symbols. At first they are not easily shared. Then, with growing language skills, they shift from expressions of self-fulfillment to vehicles for shared communication. Graphic representations, pictures that started out as scribbles, progress from lopsided ovals to regular circles to squares. Pictures of things that are at first undifferentiated scribbles to the outside observer (but not to the child) end up as accepted graphic representations.

The shift is from expressive to defined qualities. Verbal expression, which was overinclusive, where camels could be called chipmunks, where all dogs are always Fido, gradually becomes situation- and object-specific. During this period it is difficult for the child to distinguish between dreams and reality. It is not until about age seven that children realize that dreams originate in their heads and only seem to exist outside of themselves. Imagery now becomes more and more reliable and realistic, and is used to provide opportunities to practice real-life possibilities. This skill of visualization can have real value even in adult life—as, for

The Drawing of a Person

example, when we play out a scene in our heads with our boss to practice what we will say when we ask for a raise. Visualization is a skill used by many professional athletes to mentally rehearse physical skills that should come naturally when they are on the playing field. And so we come to age four when this skill, visualization, is at the apex of its development.

Signs of Development to Watch For Between Ages Three and Four

1. Is your child beginning to alternate his feet when walking down the stairs?
2. Is your child able to play with his toys without having to actively look at his hands?
3. Is your child able to hold eye contact at the 10- to 16-foot distance?
4. Does your child's language now include expressions of time, e.g., "next time," etc.?
5. Does your child show an awareness of the landmarks that he will see on trips to familiar places?
6. Does your child show the ability to visualize the results of his actions before he attempts them?

7. Is your child involved in small group activities as well as in isolated play?
8. Is your child aware of the facial expression and body language that reflect a person's mood?

Things to Do Between the Ages of Three and Four

1. Provide your child with plenty of opportunities to experience his body in all positions—balancing, rolling, tumbling.
2. As your child demonstrates good balance, begin to introduce him to scooters and roller skates.
3. This is a good age to begin to teach your child how to use simple garden and shop tools. Start with toys that function like tools, and as he demonstrates the ability to properly use the tool-toy, gradually introduce simple children's tools.
4. Play games of matching pictures. Use pictures that are very different from each other when you first start and slowly introduce pictures that are very similar except for a small detail.
5. Begin a daily read-aloud program. Have your child point to pictures that illustrate what you are reading.
6. Play a game of hide and describe. At first begin by putting two or three toys on the table and then hiding them behind a screen. Ask your child to describe what he remembers. Then uncover the toys to let him check his response. Enjoy the game and try not to preach to him. As he gets better, use pictures or designs.
7. Have your child build a simple pattern with two or three blocks. Then have him describe it to you so then you can build the pattern from his description. Slowly require accurate descriptions of shape and general placement.
8. Ask your child to act out a story that you have read to him. Allow plenty of freedom of expression.
9. Have a wind-up toy move on a table toward your child. Have your child watch the toy come to the edge of the table. As it falls off the table, have him try to catch it in a hat.

The Three-Year-Old

Motor Development

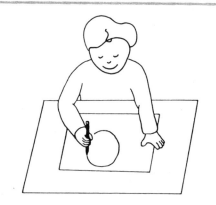

Visual Motor Development

Social Space Development

THE FOUR-YEAR-OLD

The Gang's All Here

At age four, although your child is still your baby, he or she is beginning to shed that little-boy or little-girl look. Four is an expansive age, but it slowly leads to a phase of consolidation, and then, before you can blink an eye, your child is five and off to school with the big kids. What started as the move toward independence, when he started to crawl at eight months, has led to the beginning of mental and social independence as he enters school. At that point, it will be other people who will have a large influence on his way of thinking and acting. As a parent, that thought made me somewhat sad as my boys turned four, but that year was filled with so many exciting new insights that I would have enjoyed it more had I lived for the moment instead of thinking what lay ahead. My advice to other parents is to enjoy every moment. It is a fun-filled roller-coaster ride.

Child development is a process of progressive organization, of integration. Development is like a juggling act, counterbalancing and coordinating the opposite sides of our nature, our desires, and our bodies. We have to learn how to control muscles that flex, and balance this act against the muscles that extend. We have to mediate between excitement and the inhibition of poise. We must learn to modulate the acceleration that is necessary to run for a ball with the deceleration that is necessary as we reach it and grasp it. We must learn when and how to assert ourselves, as well as when it is appropriate to withdraw. These reciprocal qualities are interwoven into a fine mesh as we proceed along the course of development. The result is a balanced form of behavior that modulates the opposites.

During the past three years, your child's behavior has alternated between being focused, where he was more alert to details and more directed toward objectives, and being peripheral, where he had a greater appreciation of the context of a situation. During his fourth year, his world will open up and expand, so that you will find him often out of bounds and peripherally oriented. But by the end of the year he will be more focused, and his behavior will be specifically directed toward an objective or a project.

Four is a year of expanding horizons in all directions. The child is now interested in a larger community, in the expansiveness of his world. His expansiveness shows up also in his imaginative play, in which he frequently conjures up new images in unreal situations. This process of visualization, along with his developing ability to be aware of the two sides of a situation, are the beginning of his growth of empathy. Visualization is the use of mental imagery to place yourself in another situation, perhaps in another person's shoes, to see the way the other fellow sees, feel the way he feels, and act the way he acts.

During this age, he is coming to the end phase of his gross motor control of opposites. When he first started his journey in life, he found it difficult to control his body as he wanted to. When an object was on the left side, he simply reached with his left hand. But if the object moved over to the right side of his body, what would he do then? He soon found that the situation called for reorienting his body, so that he could reach with his right hand, guiding it by means of his right eye. Then the day came when he was committed to reaching for an object with his right hand, and his body was already supporting that move, and all of a sudden the object crossed his midline and was closer to his left hand. What to do, what to do! This situation led him to twist his body so that the object was still on the right side of his midline. These awkward eye–hand–body contortions slowly became coordinated so that he could reach and walk with more grace. Then he had to learn how to coordinate the two sides of his body as he learned to walk up and down stairs. This puzzle was solved by going back to an earlier solution. The solution was to act as if he had only one side, and so we saw him step down with his right foot and wait there until his left foot caught up to him. Then he proceeded to the next step in the same way. And so he learned to navigate the stairs, one step at a time.

At age three and a half, he finally learned how to get the two sides of his body to cooperate as he fought the battle against gravity. What a pleasure to just freely move through space! But going down the stairs was another matter. At age four, he has finally learned to reciprocally control his body to go down the stairs. To alternate his feet must have given him the same sense of exhilaration as when Neil Armstrong stepped out onto the moon—a giant step forward.

This sense of integrated coordination of opposites will not show up as skipping until next year. Now it shows up in many other areas. For example, the child can walk while holding a cup,

Motor Development

without spilling it. He is now able to brush his teeth and button his clothes. He can coordinate his body to throw a ball quite nicely. Although he still has to learn exactly when to release the ball so he can control the height of the throw, he gets it where he wants to throw it. He is now able to combine the vertical and horizontal movements that are necessary to draw a good cross. He can run smoothly at different speeds, taking sharp corners with good stop-and-go ability. Your child's greater motor control and balance allow him to participate in more complex motor games, gymnastics, and stunts. He is now able to cooperate in group games.

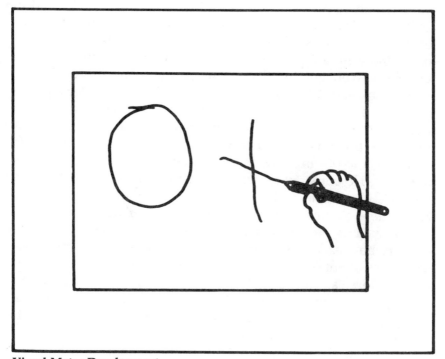

Visual Motor Development

The reciprocal integration of his two sides allows for participation in dances, and in games like Stop-and-Go and Follow the Leader. Being able to coordinate his own two sides frees him to perceive the two sides of a configuration. So not only do we now hear him asking questions about why and how, but he also begins to be aware of the attitudes and opinions of others. Though he runs hot and cold (he can love one minute and hate the next, be calm in one situation and assertive in the next, quiet now and noisy later), he can also handle his emotions by discussion now. He is also starting to learn to avoid aggression when he is angry and to look for a compromise. He is starting to understand bad and good as a consequence of what was done. You can hear the beginning of empathy as he talks about a situation and you hear him saying to himself, "Well, if I do it, then I guess he will do it." And so he begins to project himself into others. In seeking approval from his peers, he becomes more aware of how his peers feel. Play now is not only competitive, but also cooperative.

A similar development has evolved in his ability to use his vision to guide his behavior and thinking. Previously, he had to actively guide each movement. Then he developed a mental image of that movement so that his actions and thoughts were coordinated more by a replay of the memory of the necessary action than by actively guiding that action. At that point, his eyes were free to look ahead to plan the next move. Now we enter a phase of visual development when looking ahead is looking into his imagination: into the world of what might be, if . . . Thus, after a trip to the firehouse or a factory, these situations show up in his play. His role-playing now more frequently includes the feelings of others. He empathizes with his characters. When he imitates Dad, it's not just to look like Dad, but to be and feel like Dad. He is more aware of the different roles other people play. His dramatizations include familiar figures like the doctor and the delivery boy; each has his own costume and persona. He is becoming aware of others and will defend their feelings, especially other children's. This leads to having the feeling of belonging to a group. First it was belonging to a supportive mother; then to a family, possibly with siblings; and then to a very special friend; and now to a community of friends.

Your child's play with friends is often defined with commands and taboos, with out-group and in-group clearly indicated. What is developing here is the nature of a social or community group. As your child expands his visual world, he seems to need more space for his play. But he must be watched very carefully, because his new sense of space does not always conform to the previously accepted safe boundaries of yards or streets. He is apt to wander off to visit neighbors. This is an age that prepares him for being open to new situations, for understanding the pleasure of growth, and for creative ways of looking at the world.

As your child approaches his fifth year, he is being prepared to learn adult things in an adult world, in an adult manner. He has had adequate preparation, starting shortly before birth, when he began to coordinate his vision with his posture. This visual-postural coordination slowly grew so that it allowed him to balance his body as he reached for things. It also helped to keep him on the right course as his eyes and body worked together to maintain his orientation when out for a walk with Mom or when playing games with his friends. And now he will call upon this eye-body skill to help him orient himself in the classroom situation. Shortly after birth, he demonstrated the ability to sporadically keep his eyes on a movement in his visual field. This eye-tracking skill slowly developed to the point where he could keep his attention on an object and know where it is, where it is going, and when it will get there. As a result, he found that it was easier to catch a ball. He also found it easier to follow an animated discussion. When your child goes to school, he will need good visual tracking skills so that he doesn't lose his place when he reads or writes. This ability to continually pay attention visually is also necessary when the teacher presents some information at the front of the class.

The child's acuity development first allowed him to have eye contact at 8 inches. Now he is easily able to see a human eye at

Peripheral Awareness

20 feet. This means he can maintain eye contact with a teacher at the front of the classroom. He can hold his involvement with the teacher's words, body language, and ideas.

And so he is now ready to move into a new adultlike world. A world where others—not the family—will influence his developing perception. That first school bus ride is often more difficult for the parents than for the child. He was once your baby, but he is now your little boy.

Signs of Development to Watch For Between the Ages of Four and Five

1. Your child should be able to carry a container of contents, while walking, without spilling the contents.
   He should also be able to walk up steps alternating his feet. He may need a little help in the beginning.
2. He should now be able to draw a recognizable circle, a cross, and begin to draw at least three sides of a square.
3. Your child should now be able to hold eye contact out to 16 feet and by age five, out to 20 feet.
4. He should be able to accurately judge where things are in space. He can demonstrate this by building a tower of ten blocks and by tossing a ball, underhand, to you anywhere from 3 feet to 12 feet.
5. He should be able to identify objects by their color, size, and position, relative to another object.
6. He should be able to tell what street he lives on and also be able to describe something of his house.
7. He should be able to play cooperatively with a group of friends and be able to follow the rules of their game.
8. He should be able to understand how others feel in a variety of everyday situations.
9. He should be able to hold eye contact at 20 feet and follow instructions given to him at that distance.

Things to Do
Between the Ages of Four and Five

1. Take trips around your community. As you see interesting landmarks, take instant pictures. When you get home, have your child describe the trip and use the pictures to tell his story. Help him to organize his thoughts and the sequence of events.
2. Read fables to your child and later let him act out the story or else use finger paints to make a picture about the story.
3. Give your child responsibility to complete a task around the house. Give him some short simple instructions of what you want, the tools to use, and the sequence in which to use them. Reward his efforts. Correction should be accomplished by watching you perform the task next time. Let him learn by watching rather than by verbal criticisms.
4. This is a good age to begin to learn how to care for another living thing. You can start with a small plant that requires little care, or a small pet. A pet will require help from Mom or Dad.
5. Provide materials that stimulate his vivid imagination. Boxes and cartons can be used for a play store or castle.
6. A simple instant camera, Kodak or Polaroid, can be used to play pretend photographer. The pictures can be used to make an album.
7. Try the game Create a Story. It's like the game Telephone. One person starts the story, the other takes his turn continuing or finishing it.
8. Simple card games or board games help develop eye-hand coordination as well as planning and visualization.
9. A regular time for being read to will provide benefits for years to come. This is a good age for humorous stories.

The Four-Year-Old

Motor Development

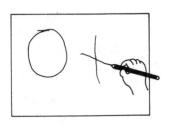

Visual Motor Development

Binocular Development

Social-Peripheral Awareness Development

4
Entering School: Age Five

Off to School with the Big Boys

The big day arrives and your child is off to school. It is interesting how frequently we have children start formal education at age five. They appear ready to learn at about that age— at least formally. They like to be part of a group. They look up to authority figures and absorb what authority figures have to say.

Their visual acuity has developed so that they demonstrate 20/20 acuity, which means, in effect, that they can see an eye at 20 feet. So they are now ready to relate to a person at the usual classroom distance. Because of this, we assume that they are fully prepared to participate in the classroom. Well, some are, and some are not. They have come a long way in five years. But what skills does the classroom situation require, and what skills do they have?

Aside from visual acuity, children entering school must be able to balance their bodies comfortably so that they can sit still and attend to what is presented. This involves an integration between their balance mechanism and their visual attention mechanism. You have seen this grow over the years so that they can sit and watch without being pulled into the action by what they are watching. The skill of sitting in a balanced posture, oriented to a learning situation and ready to absorb information, depends on the ability to balance the body while sitting and listening, reading and writing. This is the same reciprocal motor skill that the children have developed over the last five years. It started with rolling over and progressed to creeping and walking, and finally demonstrated itself when they could alternate their feet while walking down the stairs without help, or demonstrated the ability to skip. What the child really demonstrated is the reciprocal control of opposite actions of the nervous system and the muscles that position the body. They coordinate the left-side muscles with the right-side muscles, front with back, the visual cues of being upright with the postural cues of being upright. All of these co-ordinated movements are, we hope, skillfully developed so that no conscious or unconscious effort is needed to sustain coordination. If this is the case, then the child is posturally orientated to the task with minimal distraction, and is able to pay full attention to what is being presented.

Children who have not fully completed these developmental tasks are constantly reorienting themselves or are frequently seen to be fidgeting. They are constantly distracted and are unable to pay attention to what is presented. Sometimes you see children who want to pay attention so badly that they compensate by increasing the intensity of their attention. These are children who are tense, constantly chew things, and fatigue readily. They attend so intently that they frequently do not see the entire presentation or hear the entire discussion. When asked to do something, they need the instruction to be broken down into small steps, and then they need that instruction to be repeated several times. Another necessary skill is to visually monitor what is going on in the environment. For this, children need smoothly working ocular tracking skills.

One ocular tracking skill is called *pursuit tracking,* which is the ability to maintain visual attention on some ongoing activity in the visual field. When you have your child's eyes examined, this is one of the tests your optometrist will perform. A target object will be slowly moved back and forth in front of your child's eyes. It will also be moved up and down, diagonally, and in a circular movement. What is being tested is the interaction of the six little muscles that surround the eye. The optometrist wants to find out whether your child is free from any damage or interference in the neural control centers of these muscles. Also, he or she wants to know whether the muscle is free from any physical damage. Having determined that your child is free from any organic damage, the optometrist will next attend to the quality of the movement of your child's eyes. At this age, your child should easily be able to pay attention to the moving object without the need to move his head, jaw, or body. He should be able to visually pay attention and carry on a conversation at the same time. If you observe carefully, you will notice that your child's eyes do not move very smoothly. Instead, they move with small stops and starts, but they never lose attention to the moving target. This is a normal response for a five-year-old. Eye-tracking skills are not perfectly smooth until approximately the age of seven. Eye-tracking skills are a necessary component of attention behavior. They allow a person to isolate an area of space, or an object in space for visual interest and visual absorption. This skill is critically important when attending to a ball flying through the air so that it can be caught. It is also an important skill for keeping one's place when reading. It helps schoolchildren follow an animated, ongoing discussion at the front of the room. Children who have not fully developed appropriate eye-tracking skills have difficulty catching a ball, frequently lose their place when reading, and have trouble following a teacher who is demonstrating a concept with gestures and objects. There is a piecemeal quality to their perception.

Along with pursuit eye-tracking skills, there are *saccadic eye-movement* skills. Saccadic eye-movements are demonstrated when you shift your attention from one place in space to another, from

Public Space

one word to the next in reading, from one person to the other in a conversation, or from one pole on a slalom course to the next in skiing. Some children have difficulty when they overestimate the distance from one object to the next one that they will pay attention to. You can see this when they visually overshoot the mark and then have to readjust their eyes. Others have difficulty letting their attention go in order to shift from one area of attention to another. Difficulty in saccadic visual skills shows up as difficulty in making smooth transitions and in shifting attention.

A third skill necessary in the classroom is the skill of *binocular teaming*, of coordinating one eye with the other. This skill started its development around the age of six months as the child learned to aim both eyes at an object he was interested in. He learned to hold his eyes aimed at that object as he reached out to grasp it so as to inspect it. As development progressed, this binocular skill continued its development at increasing distances from the child. Interestingly enough, the place in space at which binocular skills completed their development was often the spatial distance at which the child maintained continous attention to objects and ultimately to people. Binocular skills appear, therefore, to serve the purpose of locating an area of space for involvement. As visual attention is maintained, the child concentrates on what he is looking at and develops a relationship with that object or person.

Binocular skills therefore help people locate objects in space and maintain their attention so that a relationship can develop. In school, binocular skills tend to predict the child's skills in the perception of physical objects in space. These skills make possible a freedom from clumsiness, from bumping into objects. Children with poor binocular skills frequently place objects inaccurately, as when trying to put one block on top of another, or they may show their difficulty when trying to pour liquid into a cup. During physical games, poor binocular skills show up as difficulty in catching and in batting. With diligence and practice, these errors can be masked from outside observers unless they know where to look. For example, a person works hard at athletic skills and often appears skillful, but if you watch the difference between his ability to catch a ground ball versus a fly ball, you may see that the fly ball is more difficult for him. This is also true of the tennis player when you compare his back court return with his net returns. The commonality in these examples is the possibility of misjudging the distance at which the ball is located. The closer to the ground, the less the probability of error in making a distance judgment. The ground helps indicate where the ball is in space.

This brings to mind a young man I examined several years ago. Although he had no specific complaints about his athletic skills, I questioned him very closely about his catching skills. He was very certain that he was a superb outfielder. We said goodbye in a very friendly manner after the examination. Several weeks later, I received a rather irate call from him. He accused me of talking him into poor performance as an outfielder. I asked him to return to the office so that I could ascertain what had happened. The findings of the second examination were similar to the previous one. I then asked whether he might have acquired any new habits in the interim, whether he was worried about something, or whether he had undergone any physical or medical changes. We discussed which glove he was using. The only change that had occurred was a change from right field to left field. I agreed that catching a ball in one field was the same as catching a ball in another field—that is, until he told me that when he played right field, he was facing the bleachers, and so the ball was seen against that background. When he played left field, the ball was seen against the background of the sky. Binocular skills help you locate where an object is in space. The more efficient the binocular skills, the less support you need from other perceptual sources.

In this patient's case, his poor binocular skills were masked by determination, hard work, and fortuitous placement in a situation that helped him to support his spatial judgments (in this case, the background of the bleachers helped to define where the ball was in space, or at least, where it was not).

Keeping the eyes aimed on an object helps to support sustained concentration. If a child has difficulty in maintaining eye coordination, then we will frequently see this revealed in his behavior and in his difficulty sustaining concentration and interest in reading, especially after the third grade. He will show fatigue, or loss of attention, or skipping lines when reading and difficulty in finishing assigned tasks. If he is highly motivated and continues to push himself, then he will report discomfort and headaches, eyeaches, or backaches, blurring of vision, and at times double vision. The symptoms of distractability and discomfort are really an indirect measure of motivational drive in a high-demand situation, where the child does not have the natural physiological skills to perform well. In the upper grades, when you have a bright child with good language skills and high motivation, binocular skills get masked unless you look at the disparity between scores on untimed and timed tests. Children with poor binocular skills often perform poorly on timed tests, as compared with untimed tests, because they are working hard to maintain their visual attention and are not free to easily move from one word to the next, one line to the next, or even one thought to the next. This artificially depresses their scores because they read more slowly and therefore do not answer enough questions to obtain a better score. When they take an untimed test, their scores more often reflect their mental and comprehensive abilities. These unfortunate children often do not pursue higher education in the hard sciences, even though their intelligence and interests indicate abilities in these areas, because of the frustration in demonstrating their true potential on competitive examinations. I have seen thousands of adolescents and adults who did not recognize this relationship. When it was pointed out, many elected to correct the problem and change their academic direction or jobs so they could pursue lifelong dreams that were repressed for fear of failure. Unfortunately, others could not overcome the fear of failure that had been reinforced for many years, not only during academic life, but also in a competitive workplace. This is truly a sad untold story.

Still another skill that is important in the classroom is *focusing* ability. Focusing on details allows one to distinguish between different configurations. In the beginning of reading, it allows children to distinguish between words like *hit* and *kit* or *these* and *those*. Initially, focusing developed at three months and provided the means to focus on the mother's eyes, to sustain a relationship. Although it may have been the catalyst for the beginning of affect relationships, its major developmental trend, except for its role in eye contact, has been to aid cognitive development by focusing on the attributes of objects: the qualities of hard, soft, round, square, and so on. In time, this skill links up with language, so that as the child focuses on the similarities and differences of objects and situations, he begins to label those visual experiences. Slowly, whole categories of experiences become organized. Speaking is one way of sharing one's inner image with another person. Language helps to extract the most common attributes of what was perceived so that it can be shared with another person. Slowly language transcends the image quality and develops levels of abstraction that are not directly relatable to the physical situation.

The beginning of this integration of focusing on objects and labeling the attributes appears to be built right into the nervous system. Within the nervous system there are cells that we call *feature detectors*. Some feature detectors can only recognize a horizontal line, others only vertical or diagonal lines. Still others will only respond when they see a round shape or a shape that is moving rather than one which is sitting still.

This is, in effect, the nervous system's language. However, in order for this neural language to be useful, your child must have experiences with each of these possibilities and he must pay attention while he is experiencing different shapes and orientations. Lastly, he must do something with what he experiences in order for him to use this neural language at a later time. If he hasn't had the opportunity to try to fit a square peg into a round hole and then changed to a round peg, he may later have difficulty seeing the difference between pet and pot.

Before your child can be successful in learning to read words in a book, he will have had to learn to read the lines, shapes, and angles that he sees everyday. In this way he is able to understand many things that he has never actually dealt with before. Visual language becomes the means of understanding the feel, smell, taste, and shape of things. This is how all forms of language develop. It is the means of conveying information from one sense into the vocabulary of another. Each of these perceptual labels is then combined into whole new categories of objects such as chair, table, or car. In this way he becomes able to understand things that he may never have dealt with before.

In the beginning, all four legged animals were "Doggie," even cats and horses. After a while, he can recognize which animal at the zoo is the camel based on a previous description. Learning to see takes time. It is not enough to look, he must learn to selectively focus. Learning to see is learning to understand or comprehend. It is very much like learning to read. In reading we require that the child be aware that there is something visually available for him to relate to. He must focus on what is important. In fact, learning to read assumes that your child has learned to see in a meaningful way—in effect, that he has developed his vision.

Hopefully, after reading these chapters you will not take his vision development for granted. In order to ensure that he is fully prepared for school, make sure that he has a complete vision examination and not just a check of his ability to read the eye chart. A complete examination should include tests that are performed at your child's reading distance (at approximately 12 to 16 inches) as well as at the far point of vision (at 20 feet).

The following areas should be evaluated:

1. Visual acuity
2. Eye health
3. Eye movement abilities
4. Focusing ability
5. Binocular coordination
6. Eye-hand coordination
7. Form and spatial perception

Is Your Child Ready for School?

Your child should *not* show any of the following. If he does, have your optometrist examine him before he goes to school.

1. Crusts on his lids or red eyelids.
2. Styes or swollen lids.
3. Watery eyes or mucus discharge.
4. Red eyes.
5. Sensitivity to light.
6. Eyes that do not look coordinated.
7. Rubbing his eyes.
8. Complaints of itching or a burning sensation in his eyes.
9. Complaints of discomfort when doing close visual tasks, e.g., coloring, solving puzzles, reading, etc.
10. Tense or distorted posture of the body when viewing objects.
11. Squinting or blinking.
12. Holding a book too far or too close or continual adjustment of the distance. (The proper distance that a book or object requiring critical attention should be held can be determined by measuring his forearm. The distance between his elbow and his knuckles is the approximate distance that he should hold a book from his eyes.)
13. Confusion of similar letters, *o* and *e, m* and *n, f* and *t*. (Confusion of reversible letters such as *p, g, d,* and *b* is common when children first enter school but it should not be present, except rarely, by age six and a half.)

Your Child Should Be Able to Demonstrate the Following:

1. Be able to work alone without continuous encouragement.
2. Be able to follow through and complete a task when working alone.
3. Have sufficient attention skills to sit relatively quietly, without squirming or needing to get up to run around, for approximately 10 to 15 minutes.

4. He should be able to describe what he sees.
5. He should be able to coordinate his body in activities such as stripping and dressing himself.
6. He should be able to read or follow a story in a book with his eyes alone, without having to move his head or use his finger.
7. He should be able to demonstrate that he sees a whole shape when copying simple geometric patterns such as a square. He should only have to look once to copy a square, not once for each line.
8. When copying figures, he should orient at least the first three in a left to right manner.
9. He should be able to do continuous close work without having to close or block one eye.
10. He should be able to write his name in a relatively straight line and not have letters on different lines.

The Five-Year-Old

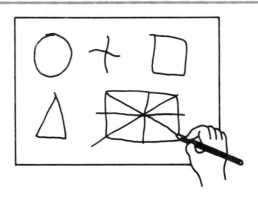

Visual Motor Development

Public Space
Social-Peripheral Awareness Development

PART TWO:

VISION AND
THE ENVIRONMENT

5
Vision and the Learning-Disabled Child

If the key to a better society is education, then the key to a better education is better vision.

—Lucy Johnson Nugent

Dyslexia

What is it that happens to these children? They grow up, have fun, make friends, and laugh all the time. Then they get to school and become different children. They become withdrawn or aggressive, bite their nails, wet their beds. It is as if the stitching that held them together has become unraveled, and they fall apart. They don't smile anymore. They have outbursts. They stop communicating. Before you know it, you are running to school for conferences. The notes sent home become more strident. New doctors and professionals become a part of your life. It appears that the turbulence of growth is nothing compared with the confusion and frustration you now feel. At least during the early growth years, each stage was followed by spurts of development, maturity, and stability. This combination merry-go-round and steeplechase results in a never-ending cycle downward. "Why did this happen to me?" The answer comes back: because you are the parent of a dyslexic or learning-disabled child.

What is a learning disability? According to the Learning Disabilities Act (1969), it is

> A disorder in one or more of the basic psychological processes involved in understanding or in using spoken or written language. These may be manifested in disorders of listening, thinking, talking, reading, writing, spelling or arithmetic. They include conditions which have been referred to as perceptual handicaps, brain injury, minimal brain disfunction, dyslexia, developmental aphasia, etc. They do not include learning problems which are primarily due to visual (the need for eyeglasses to see clearly), hearing or motor handicaps (cerebral palsy), mental retardation, emotional disturbance or environmental disadvantage.

Did you know that 25 percent of the adult population have difficulty arriving at correct conclusions when they read conflicting statements? Did you know that 15 percent have difficulty answering questions about the daily TV schedule that they have already read? Did you know that 13 percent of adults have difficulty when they go to fill out an application form for a loan? You may have heard that more paperback books were being sold now than ever before. But have you also heard that 75 percent of the books sold are bought by the same 10 percent of the population?

Being able to read well is not a luxury; it is an essential need. Despite the great advances in technology, the preponderance of TV, and the onslaught of computers, higher levels of education and specialized training are being required today of almost everybody. Basic to these increasing levels of education is the ability to read adequately. If you wanted to become an army cook, you would be required to be able to read at the seventh-grade level.

To do repair work requires eighth-grade reading abilities in order to deal with repair manuals.

Yet approximately 15 percent of children in the United States have sufficient difficulty in reading for us to label them learning-disabled. That means that anywhere from seven to eight million children suffer as a result of this disability. The percentage of learning-disabled children varies as we go from country to country. In Japan, only 1 percent are learning-disabled. In Sweden, the figure is 8 percent. In England, it's 10 percent. If we went to Argentina, we'd find 14 percent, and in Austria, it would be 22 percent.

Over the years, many theories have been proposed to explain learning disabilities. These have included brain damage, perceptual problems, attentional problems, allergic reactions, and developmental lags. Although there has been considerable discussion regarding the causes and treatments of learning disabilities, the situation still remains, for most people, confused and controversial.

In my opinion, too much time and energy have been spent trying to determine the cause of the condition. The search for the cause, in order to pin an exact label on children who are under-achieving, has only led to dividing professionals instead of fostering a collaboration that is necessary to help these children function more appropriately. When we discuss children with learning disabilities, we must use descriptions that reveal an insight into their mental and perceptual processes: descriptions that help to generate usable services. All too often, the labels that are applied become self-fulfilling prophecies.

Over the course of my twenty-five years of clinical practice, I have treated a wide range of children who have been labeled severely retarded, autistic, brain-injured, emotionally disturbed, deaf, underachievers, and dyslexic. Although the labeling process may have been helpful to obtain educational funds, I have found it more productive to consider these children as falling somewhere on a continuum of learning *ability*, each one showing an individual learning style. There are no perfect minds. Each child has a different style of learning. Some are better at one task and poorer at another. Not only are there different styles, but the pace of learning also differs among children. Among adults, these differences can be dealt with more easily because of the large range of occupations that they have to choose from. An adult can use his style productively by carefully selecting his occupation. The child, on the other hand, has only one occupation: school. That occupation requires very specific behaviors at very specific times. Distracted and imaginative behavior in a child can be a discomfort to the harried teacher. But for the adult who has chosen a creative field, it can be a source of great pride and rich rewards.

Not every child can easily fit into this artificial, but necessary, regime. But that does not necessarily mean that a maladaptive style of learning should be considered a disease or psychiatric disorder. After all, if that were the case, we would never have seen Albert Einstein grow up to become such a productive member of society. Einstein, during his early school years, displayed very similar kinds of imaginative and disruptive behavior. If the term were used during that time, he would have been labeled a learning-disabled child. It is more productive to view each style as a variation, sometimes as a deviation or delay in the child's development.

The child should be treated sympathetically and with loving, warm support to allow him to feel that he is wanted and accepted as a person. The obstacles that impede his progress should be dealt with in a matter-of-fact way, much the same as you would clear the table in order to sit down to eat. Labels and blame should not be a part of the process.

Just because we start to introduce reading at age six does not mean that every child will profit, no matter how skilled the instruction. Many reading problems stem from the fact that children's maturation rates differ, yet instruction is started despite this developmental fact. For some children, it would be better if they were held over during the very early years. However, this should not be a waiting game. Children who are maturing slowly should be given increased opportunities to enhance their perceptual and other readiness skills. Others, who are developing slowly, can profit from special instruction which is geared to their pace.

In 1975, I helped develop just such a program, which was used in one of the New York City school districts. It was my belief then, and continues to be even more strongly now, after much experience, that all children are programmed to learn. Learning about themselves and their world is as much a part of their lives as eating. The differences among children lie primarily in style, pace, and in ability to assimilate what is learned. I feel strongly that any child who otherwise demonstrates what we might call normal intelligence has the ability to learn to read, write, and do arithmetic. What he needs is a sympathetic teacher who is skilled in presenting material in an individualized manner. The child also needs an environment that is conducive to his learning style. If he is distractable, then he needs a room environment that limits the tumult which is frequent in a class of thirty-five. He also needs a well organized, structured presentation of materials. In order to profit from the teacher and the classroom situation, he needs to be helped to develop the attentional, perceptual, and language skills that are a prerequisite for learning.

The program that I developed incorporated these very ideas. A test battery was organized to determine the levels of ability that the children had developed. One area that I felt was very important was the ability to inhibit extraneous movement so that the child could pay attention to information that was being presented. For this, we looked very carefully at each child's body coordination. We measured his ability to visually steer his body through space as well as coordinate the two sides of his body (bilateral coordination). Children below school age, or immature school-age children, tend to show behaviors that are not conducive to classroom learning. They tend to be drawn physically toward something that catches their eyes and ears, or they do not visually monitor and guide their actions, and so they often wind up doing something other than what they set out to do. Because they have not yet learned to coordinate the two sides of their body, they tend to fidget and to show generally clumsy behavior.

We also evaluated the visual-perceptual and visual skills areas. Here the child had to judge shapes that were similar and dissimilar to other shapes. The ability to discern shapes is important when children have to recognize different letters that look alike, such as G and C, B and E, or M and N. It is also necessary when they have to judge lookalike words such as *bat* and *bet*. It is important to be able to recognize the same letter or letter combination each time that they see it in order to attach the correct sound, so that they will be able to say what they see.

We also included tests in which the child had to demonstrate his ability to recognize the position of objects in space. This ability is important when the child has to discriminate between *b* and *d*, or *on* and *no*, or *was* and *saw*.

The visual skills that we measured included eye-tracking skills, which told us about the child's ability to know where he is (visual attending), and whether he is able to sustain that attention when he must move his eyes to understand what is going on. We measured his ability to focus his eyes and to shift that focus appropriately. (Focusing skills are important when a child must follow information the teacher presents at the front of the room and must then shift his attention to his paper or books.) The child's eye-teaming skills were also evaluated so that we would know if he could judge where things were in space in relationship to himself and could maintain continued visual attention without distraction.

The third area that we evaluated was the child's language skills and auditory perception. These skills are crucially important, especially when we wanted to know whether a child who mislabeled a picture did so because he misjudged what it looked like, or because he didn't have the appropriate words in his vocabulary, or because he was unable to pronounce the words that he did know.

When all the information was gathered, we sat down as a team—optometrist, teacher, psychologist, paraprofessional, and others—and developed an individualized program for each child. Some parts of the program were geared for use within the regular classroom, and some parts were to be used by a separate resource teacher. Some children had to be referred to outside vision specialists.

Children who took part in this program were first- and second-grade children from two different schools. Before the program started, all children were given standardized reading and achievement tests. (The same tests were given to a control group of children.) After six weeks, the children were retested. Some very significant changes had occurred. Aside from the statistically significant increases in word reading and sentence reading, there were other profound changes in many children. They looked better and they performed better in terms of paying attention and generally seemed more focused on their tasks. We were all in agreement that the children now appeared ready to learn. It didn't take much, except cooperation among the professionals involved, time, and money to support the program. Unfortunately, what happened afterward is what happens all too often in education. A budget crisis comes, followed by a change in priorities. And so the children who needed help were left out, while professionals continued to debate the proper terminology for their conditions so that a magic bullet could be found that would cure all of their symptoms.

In order to truly help learning-disabled children, we have to look at each child individually. That's not easy in a class of thirty-five when all of the children have to follow the same curriculum. We must decide whether each child has to fit into the mold that we define, or whether we are willing to alter the school situation to meet individual childrens' needs. My suggestion to parents is to start now, before your child goes to school. Learn to recognize the developmental lags that may spell problems later on. Provide activities that stimulate development of those perceptual skills that will be needed in the classroom, and, most important, find a vision specialist skilled in child development who can help you to accomplish these goals (see chapter 13).

The best time to provide help for a child is during the pre-school years. All children should be evaluated regularly by a behavioral optometrist as well as by a pediatrician. I would recommend a first evaluation at six months of age, and then an evaluation every six months until age three. Thereafter, I would suggest a yearly schedule unless you or the doctor observes some questionable behavior or development.

Often, delays seen when a child is very young can be dealt with very simply. Most children have fluctuations and unevenness in their development. However, if any skill or area is persistently delayed by greater than 25 percent, then some simple intervention is warranted. A 25 percent delay means that a four-year-old skill is performed at a three-year-old level. A skill that should be present at three years still remains at the level of two years and four months, and so on. (See table of developmental lags, page 105.)

Providing enhancement activities during the early years can aid a child's development. In this way, he will have a greater chance of success when he enters school.

Learning to read is very similar to learning to see with comprehension. When we are learning to see, we develop a visual vocabulary. The lines, shapes, forms, colors, and movements in our environment have a language of their own. Learning to read them and to understand them takes time for a child.

Visual objects are like a form of written language. The letters of this language are the visual sizes, shapes, positions, and movements of objects in the environment. Once your child learns this basic visual language (and in order to do so, he must learn how to pay attention), he will then understand concepts such as round, square, straight, and curved. With this knowledge, he will learn the names of new objects within the same category. These learned visual skills are the very ones we assume he has mastered when he presents himself to the reading task. If he has not truly learned these skills, he will not be ready to read. When the child learns to read, he goes through the same process. He must become aware that there's something visually available for him to deal with. Next he must be able to see it as a separate object, separate from its background. He then must identify it as part of a category or a class with one or more attributes. And so he develops the ability to recognize words.

In the early school years, these perceptual skills can be developed and enhanced rather easily. If we wait until a child has experienced repeated frustration, (especially when he has already failed to master reading), we may find that the perceptual problems have become compounded by changes in attitude and behavior that make him harder to work with. The following guidelines are a means of determining whether your child is having some visual difficulties. Look them over carefully. Don't delay seeking help if any of these descriptions fit your child.

The ABCs of Vision Difficulties

A. **Appearance**
   1. Closing of one eye
   2. One eye turning in or out at any time
   3. Excessive blinking
   4. Red eyes or lids
   5. Crust on eyelids
   6. Frequent sties
   7. Squinting in normal sunlight or under fluorescent lights
   8. Frowning or squinting when paying attention visually
   9. Frequent occurrence of swollen lids
   10. Frequent tearing of eyes
B. **Behavior**
   1. Attention
      a. Difficulty staying with a visual task long enough to complete it
      b. Tendency to daydream, which disrupts the ability to do tasks correctly
      c. Tendency to fatigue during tasks requiring visual concentration

2. Eye-Tracking Ability
   a. Moves head during reading or when looking at picture books.
   b. Loses place when reading.
   c. Needs a finger or a marker to hold place.
   d. Rereads frequently.
   e. Skips lines while reading.
   f. Frequently omits small words.
   g. Miscalls the beginnings or ends of words.
   h. Uses poor spacing or orienting of words to the page when writing.
   i. Writes numbers in the wrong column.
   j. Has difficulty following the flight of a ball.
   k. Has difficulty following the sequence of printed instructions.
   l. Has difficulty solving a maze puzzle.
3. Eye-Hand Coordination
   a. Does not use eyes to guide hands when doing manual tasks.
   b. Writes or prints slowly.
   c. Has difficulty writing on ruled lines.
   d. Misaligns a series of numbers that has to be printed vertically or horizontally.
   e. Has difficulty properly connecting *t*'s or dotting *i*'s.
   f. Does poorly on tests that require marking the correct space, although he knows the answers.
   g. Avoids eye-hand activities such as catching, batting, tying laces or knots, sharpening pencils.
   h. Tends to write his name or answers to questions in a hurried manner.
   i. Avoids playing instruments that require accurate placement of fingers.
   j. Tends to close eyes or avert eyes when using tools.
4. Eye-Teaming Abilities
   a. Has difficulty judging where things are in space.
   b. Reports double vision.
   c. Repeats letters within words.
   d. Repeats small words when reading or writing.
   e. Closes or squints one eye.
   f. Misaligns numbers when writing in columns.
   g. Misaligns head or body when working at a desk or task.
   h. Tends to become distractable if required to maintain visual attention for a period of time.

    i. Has poorer scores on timed tests than he has on similar untimed tests.

    j. Continued visual attention causes increased visual discomfort.

    k. Has difficulty maintaining eye contact.

    l. Becomes disoriented or uncomfortable in crowded places.

5. Form-Perception Abilities

    a. Confuses similar geometric shapes.

    b. Has difficulty distinguishing between somewhat similar letters, such as *M* and *N*, or *H* and *N*, or *r* and *n*.

    c. Has difficulty recognizing the same word in different sentences.

    d. Confuses words with similar beginnings.

    e. Confuses words with similar endings.

    f. Has difficulty recognizing words that are written instead of printed.

    g. Dislikes collecting objects such as baseball cards and stamps.

    h. Has difficulty using a dictionary or file cards.

    i. Gets confused when required to use the correct key or tool.

    j. Misreads similar numbers.

6. Spatial-Perceptual Abilities

    a. Confuses left and right.

    b. Gets confused with spatial words—*above, below, outside, in front of*, etc.

    c. Has difficulty organizing the space on a paper.

    d. Writes crookedly or spaces poorly.

    e. Confuses words such as *on* and *no*, or *was* and *saw*, or numbers such as 12 and 21, or 6 and 9.

    f. Transposes letters of words and writes *noldon* instead of *London*.

    g. Gets confused with maps.

    h. Has difficulty reading directions; would rather plunge ahead and work it out.

    i. Has more difficulty with geometry than algebra.

    j. Tends to take the wrong turn when traveling to familiar places.

C. **Complaints**

1. Eye discomfort after concentrated visual attention
2. Headaches associated with using eyes
3. Burning of eyes

4. Itching of eyes with usage
5. Objects appearing double
6. Objects tend to blur and then clear
7. Objects or words appear to move
8. Dizziness when using eyes
9. The sensation of a film appearing over eyes
10. Printed page appears to get dull or very bright

Developmental Lags

Each item in this table is approximately 25 percent below what is normally expected. If your child demonstrates at least two items in these tables, he or she should have a developmental examination.

A. **Bilateral Integration**
1. Three Months
   a. Still lies on his back in a TNR (tonic neck reflex) posture—head facing one side, arm extended on that side as if in a fencing position.
   b. Visually follows a moving target downward but not upward.
   c. Not able to hold his head erect, even for a moment.
2. Eight Months
   a. Unable to hold trunk erect.
   b. Has not begun to move by using his arms, only attempts supporting his weight in a crawling position.
   c. There is no unilateral reaching. All reaching is still bilateral.
3. Eighteen Months
   a. Unable to walk without holding adult's hand or furniture.
   b. Not able to go up the stairs, but is able to stoop and then recover balance.
   c. Reaching and manipulating things still requires two hands in a task; not able to coordinate activity unilaterally.
   d. Not able to hold more than one object at the same time.
4. Three Years
   a. Unable to stand on one foot.
   b. Unable to alternate feet going up the stairs, but is able to walk up and down the stairs one step at a time.

       c. Unable to jump from the bottom step, but is able to kick a large ball.

       d. Unable to ride a tricycle.

  5. Four Years

       a. Unable to hop on one foot, but can balance on one foot for five seconds.

       b. Unable to walk down the steps alternating his feet. Can only do this going up the steps.

       c. Unable to carry a cup of water without spilling, but does demonstrate balanced walking, one foot directly in front of the other, as well as the ability to walk within two converging lines that are 12 inches apart at one end and 4 inches at the other.

       d. Unable to throw a ball overhead.

  6. Five Years

       a. Unable to alternate feet when skipping, although he can hop on one foot.

       b. Unable to walk backward heel to toe, but can walk forward.

       c. Unable to walk on a 10-foot, 2½-inch board without stepping off, but can walk down the stairs alternating feet.

       d. Unable to kick a soccer ball on the run, but is able to hop on one foot and is able to throw overhead.

B. Ocular Motor Skills

  1. Three Months

       a. Does not follow a moving object past the midline.

       b. Unable to follow an object upward; only downward.

       c. Regards an object moved in front of his eyes only momentarily.

  2. Eight Months

       a. Will not sustain his attention while you scribble on a paper. He's more attentive to his own actions.

       b. Convergence ability—following with both eyes an object which approaches his face—is not sustained.

       c. One eye may still cross at times (strabismus).

  3. Eighteen Months

       a. Does not watch where he is going to go, nor does he visually guide his actions.

       b. Maintains visual attention on activities occurring 3 to 5 feet from him, but not beyond.

     c. Still moves his head and body as he visually tracks the movement of an object.

4. Three Years
   a. Is able to visually attend to a moving object without moving his body, but frequently has head movements along with his eye movements.
   b. When he shifts attention from one object to another, he tends to support the eye shift with head movements.
   c. Not able to simultaneously walk and observe something happening near him; he must stop walking to look.
   d. The movements of wheels and disks still attract his attention.

5. Four Years
   a. Can only follow an object moving in toward his face up to approximately 4 to 5 inches; then he shifts his attention or moves his head away.
   b. As he follows a moving object, his eyes do not move smoothly but move in large jumps. There are some minimal head movements.
   c. Can shift his attention from one object to another without head movements, but tends to momentarily lose track of the target.
   d. When you ask him to follow an object that you are holding in your hand, he tends to shift attention to your hand.

6. Five Years
   a. Can only follow an object moving in toward his face up to 3 inches, then he looks away.
   b. Can follow a moving target without moving his head, but his eyes still move in small stops and starts.
   c. Can shift attention from one object to another but his eyes tend to overshoot or undershoot the target.

C. **Eye-Hand Coordination**
   1. Three Months
      a. Does not hold a rattle.
      b. Little or no regard for his own hand.
      c. Hands may still be fisted.
   2. Eight Months
      a. Does not explore objects that he holds in his hand.
      b. Will reach and grasp large objects, but small pellets only elicit raking attempts.

    c. When reaching for objects, he is not able to continue holding what he already has in his hands. He must put it down.

3. Eighteen Months
   a. Not able to place one cube upon another. The release function has only developed to the point where he can release in the vicinity of the other block, not on top of it.
   b. Cannot imitate a vertical crayon stroke; only brushes crayon on the paper.
   c. Does not insert any shapes correctly on a three-piece form board.

4. Three Years
   a. Unable to place at least four blocks on a ten-piece form board, but is able to complete all three pieces of a three-piece form board.
   b. Does not copy a circle; only makes horizontal strokes.
   c. Can build a tower of five to six cubes but is unable to build a train with a chimney.
   d. Unable to fold and crease a paper.

5. Four Years
   a. Still must watch carefully what he does with his hands.
   b. Can correctly place only four blocks on a ten-piece form board.
   c. Can only copy a circle and approximate a cross.
   d. Is unable to build a bridge with cubes; only builds a train with a chimney.

6. Five Years
   a. Builds a bridge with blocks.
   b. Can copy a circle or cross; makes a square look like a capital *D*.
   c. Unable to copy a triangle.
   d. Can place only eight pieces on a ten-piece board.

D. Space Perception: Direction

1. Eighteen Months
   a. Uses no spatial words.
   b. Unable to consistently put cubes in a cup.
   c. Unable to respond to the question, "Where do you want to go?"

2. Two Years
   a. Spatial vocabulary is confined to *up* and *down*.

    b. Answers the question "Where do you go with your mother?" only by looking or pointing, not by any description.

    c. Unable to fit two halves of a sphere together to make a ball.

3. Three Years

    a. Spatial vocabulary does not include words such as *over, from, by, on top of,* but does include *there, where, in, out, turn around.*

    b. Unable to place an object as directed under or next to a chair, but can give it to mother or place it on the chair.

    c. When asked where mother is, can only answer, "In the house," not specify a place in the house, like the kitchen.

4. Four Years

    a. Unable to follow directions when told to place a toy: on, in, behind, in front, beside.

    b. Not able to distinguish front and back of clothing.

    c. Unable to fit three shapes together to make a design.

    d. Unable to copy a sequence of four beads, blocks, or objects.

5. Five Years

    a. Unable to put two triangles together to make a rectangle.

    b. Unable to put toys away in an orderly fashion.

    c. Does not know his left or right side.

    d. Not able to place a mark correctly in a drawing when told to place it under, above, behind, or in front of a printed shape. Only gets one placement correct.

6
Vision at Play: Toys and Games

Adults work; children play. That statement seems to imply that play is frivolous, but is it really? Play is universal among the young of higher primates as well as children. It surely must serve a useful purpose. Scientists have noted that chimpanzees use special facial expressions to indicate, "I want to play. How about you?" If another chimpanzee does not see the signal, it is liable to conclude that a play fight is a real fight. If it sees the signal, then the pretend fight can begin. Playing is a way that animals have of practicing skills that they may need at other times. Jerome Bruner, discussing the work of Jane Van Lawick-Goodall, at the Gombe Stream Reserve in Tanzania, tells the story of how chimpanzees learn a useful game from their elders. The game is called "termiting." In this game, chimpanzees wet a stick with their mouths and then place it into a termite hole. After a while, they remove the stick, which is now coated with termites to be eaten. For chimpanzees, this is a very rewarding activity. After carefully observing this activity among adults, young chimpanzees play at selecting sticks of the appropriate length. Then they learn to strip the stick of its leaves. Finally, when they have put all the parts of the game together, they have learned to fish for termites.

When I read Goodall's work, I was reminded of what my sons went through when they were learning how to fish. One day I watched one of them coordinate his body beautifully as he cast his line out into the lake. A fish took to his line immediately, but his face told another story. The fishing line had gotten all tangled up—it looked like a plate of spaghetti. The frustration that was evident at that time was painful to watch. It brought home to me the need for the preparation that is necessary to be able to play. Having fun at play sometimes requires that the child have mastery of the necessary skills so that he can leave his play feeling good, happy, and alive. Developing those skills is what early play is all about. It provides the opportunity to practice simple behaviors that are later combined into sophisticated, skillful actions. When we see a child throw an object and then go to search for it, we are witnessing his learning not only of spatial-perceptual skills, but also of scanning, focusing, and aiming his eyes. When a child grabs an object and then watches it as he guides it into his mouth, he is practicing eye-hand coordination skills, and he is learning to coordinate his two eyes as he directs them toward the object in his hand. In all of these situations, visual skills are being learned by the child, often without our realizing it. The learning appears to occur so naturally that the child seems to need no help. But that is not true. He needs a conducive environment, things to play with and explore, and he often needs someone to interact with who will encourage his experimentation.

Play starts very naturally. Babies, when they are satisfied after being nursed, will often play with the mother's nipple. This is true for babies who are bottle-fed as well. If you watch them, you will see the enjoyment they have as they roll the nipple around with their tongue. It doesn't take much time before mother naturally responds by playing with baby's fingers and toes. As your baby grows in this mutually playful manner, you will find that he soon plays with you by pushing and by pulling and by swiping. What you are witnessing is his trying out new forms of contact with his environment. As he enjoys this contact and as he is encouraged to continue it, he begins to explore his new world. Your baby has a built-in need to explore his new world. It is an age-old survival need. To be successful in his explorations, he needs two things. First, he needs opportunities through play that help to stimulate and enhance his developing visual abilities so that he can explore his new environment. If he has objects that attract his attention, he will practice looking. The first thing he is impelled to look at is a configuration of hairline, eyes, and mouth—especially the eyes, and especially if they are his mother's eyes, which then smile back at him. Once this pleasurable form of looking is stimulated, your baby will need other objects with patterns in them to stimulate continued growth of looking and focusing on details.

Shortly, play needs shift to manipulating those objects that the baby sees. At this point, he needs objects to reach out to so that he can finger and mouth them. He is now practicing using his visual system to guide his hands as he reaches. Then he compares what he sees with what he feels and how it tastes. In order for reaching to be accurate, he needs to develop cooperation between his two eyes so that they point to the same place in space and tell him the location of a desired toy. Continued exploration of his environment requires continued development of his visual skills. René Spitz says, "Vision is a gift which integrates stimulations of taste, audition, smell and touch." Vision is also the searchlight and the radar device that actively guides our exploration. Playthings and play opportunities provide the fertile ground for those skills to develop. A second important ingredient which fosters continued development is something or someone to interact with. The first important someone is a parent or other caregiver. Your baby needs someone to encourage playfulness. It is this playful interaction that sparks his curiosity to explore. Without that spark, play, instead of being the medium of learning how to learn, can become the means of learning how *not* to learn. It is the affective interchange between a mother and her child that awakens curiosity and makes learning desirable and allows the child to feel capable. Spitz has shown, with his studies of children reared in institutions, that when children do not have this interaction, although they are well fed, they stop reaching out and become apathetic. Not only does perceptual growth stop, but life itself can be threatened in this type of situation. As a child's curiosity is encouraged, he begins to explore the perceptual attributes of his world and how he can use his body to gain access to that experience. His games start off as a primitive means of exploring sensory experiences for the immediate gratification he receives. They progress to creating new ways of playing which soon require more than the elementary motor and sensory skills. "First I put this mobile in my mouth. Boy, it tastes so good. Next

I pull on it so that it shimmers and jingles a bell. It tickles my insides. Now I see that if I pull on this mobile, I can reach that one. Goody, goody. I wonder if I can get that toy over there by pulling on this string the way I pulled on the other one."

Children play in order to learn about themselves and their environment. Then they use that learning to control their environment. In the early years, when visual skills are being developed, toys and games can be a potent means of helping to stimulate and enhance vision development.

TOYS AND GAMES TO AID VISION DEVELOPMENT

Dr. Baxter Swarthout tells a story of the research that the Joseph P. Kennedy Foundation supported in the area of mental retardation. It is a story of how two psychologists changed the environment of retarded infants from that of a sterile, institutional setting to an environment rich in personal interaction, handling, toys to manipulate, and visual games to play. Twenty-five years later, the two psychologists were presented with awards for their outstanding work, which had made people aware that inheritance cannot be considered a barrier to leading a productive life. The awards were presented by one of those very same infants that they had worked with. He now was leading a normal life, with a wife and three children. He, incidentally, holds a master's degree in public administration. Obviously, not many retarded children are likely to repeat this story, but it is a potent reminder to us not to be too quick to condemn a child to an unproductive life just because his growth was below the norm. Providing an active environment, which is rich in the possibilities of multiple interactions, can allow children to maximize their potential.

Toys are a very useful means of stimulating your child's vision development. However, they also provide the possibility of harm. Make sure that the toys you buy are not so small that they can be swallowed or put into a nose or an ear. The Toy Manufacturers of America recommend that you use the following guidelines when you purchase toys:

1. Read the labels for any safety precautions.
2. Throw away plastic wrappings so that your child does not use them inappropriately.

3. With infants and with very young children, do not use toys with string or cord that can cause strangulation.
4. Make sure that projectiles have cork, rubber, or other forms of protective tips.
5. Broken toys that have sharp edges should be thrown out.
6. Do not use items that shoot or propel objects for young children. They may injure eyes or get stuck in throats.
7. Make sure that buttons on dolls cannot be bitten off or eaten.
8. Make sure that the toys you buy are nontoxic, flame-retardant, and flame resistant.
9. Make sure that rubber toys cannot be swallowed, even if they are compressed to their smallest size.
10. Do not leave the games of older children around if they can be harmful to younger children.

When you buy a toy, think of its possibility for developing your child's vision. The following are some suggestions and guidelines for toys and games.

Birth to Three Months
A. General Motor and Bilateral Development
1. Playfully move your baby's arms and legs, at first each part separately and then in various combinations.
2. Raise and lower your baby while you look into each other's eyes.
3. Bounce your baby gently on the bed or on your knee.
4. Gently and playfully massage the baby's body with baby lotion or powder.
5. Place multicolored mitts on the baby's hands. Make sure the material is safe for him to put in his mouth.

B. Visual Focusing
1. Place a picture of a face 8 to 12 inches from the baby's eyes. The face should be about 10 inches in diameter and the eyes in the face should be about 1 inch in diameter. Place the face on one side of the crib and change sides regularly until the age of approximately two months, and then hang it from the middle of the crib. Make sure that you place the face so that the baby has an opportunity to look toward each side of his body.
2. Hang a patterned piece of material on the crib with a bell attached to it.

3. Provide multicolored objects for your baby to look at. Place the objects in various positions within his view. Give him opportunities to look in different directions.
4. Leave a nightlight on at night, so your baby will have something to look at if he awakens.
5. Make sure that he doesn't face one side of his crib or a wall, using one eye all of the time. Change his position, or that of the crib, occasionally.
6. Hold your baby on opposite sides of your body while feeding him so that he gets a chance to use each eye for looking.

C. **Visual Tracking**
1. Hold your face about 8 to 12 inches in front of your baby, and talk and sing to him while you slowly move to one side of his body and then to the other.
2. Take a large patterned object (such as a doll or a balloon) with a bell attached, and move it in front of his face, approximately 8 to 10 inches in front of his eyes. Move the object slowly from side to side.
3. Make a bridge between the two sides of the crib and attach a multicolored object to it that can be made to swing.
4. Place a roly-poly doll approximately 8 to 12 inches in front of your baby's eyes, and set it moving.

D. **Visual-Auditory Coordination**
1. Place noisy rattles with different textures in his hands so that he can shake them and then place them in his mouth.
2. Put squeaky rubber toys in his hands.

E. **Eye-Hand Coordination**
1. Make a bridge between the two sides of the crib and hang objects there that will invite swatting. Make sure that the objects change pattern or make noise as they move.
2. Hang a cradle gym across the crib.
3. A good mobile to hang over the crib is a picture of a smiling face.

Four Months to Eight Months
A. **General Motor and Bilateral Development**
1. Holding your baby's hands, gently lift him up from the crib and then slowly lower him.
2. Place your baby face down across a round bolster. Gently roll him over until his hands touch the ground, and then roll him back until his knees touch the ground.

3. Put wrist and ankle bracelets on the baby so that he becomes aware of the movement of the two sides of his body.
4. Make climbing and sliding equipment out of stiff and smooth pillows and bolsters.
5. Place a kickable mobile at the end of the crib.
6. Place small objects within his reach, so he can practice grasping and holding abilities.

B. **Visual Focusing**
1. Place a plastic mirror (without sharp edges) in a place where your baby will catch a view of himself.
2. Place stuffed toys of different sizes and shapes and patterns around the room for him to look at.
3. Roll a patterned ball toward him as he sits on the floor.
4. Play peekaboo with your baby.
5. Hang a three-dimensional face on the crib for your baby to look at.

C. **Visual Tracking**
1. Call your baby's attention to you as you creep behind a piece of furniture and then emerge from the other side.
2. Walk in front of your baby, pulling a desirable pull-toy, such as a dog on a string.
3. Jingle a set of toy keys approximately 12 inches in front of his eyes to stimulate his eye-following abilities. Do this from left to right and back and then up and down and so forth.
4. Roll objects down an incline in front of your baby so that he can watch what they do.

D. **Eye-Hand Coordination**
The following toys and objects provide multiple opportunities for exploring eye-hand coordination possibilities.
1. Nesting toys.
2. A coffee percolator.
3. Pots and pans.
4. Bangable objects, such as a drum or pounding pegs, especially large ones.
5. Tie objects onto the side of the highchair so that the baby can throw them to the floor and you can retrieve them more easily. Make sure that they make different sounds as they reach the end of the string.

E. **Two-Eye Teaming**
1. Attach toys to strings so that your baby can pull them toward himself.

2. When bathing the baby, provide toys that can float toward and away from him.
3. Play a choo-choo game with some food as it goes into his tunnel of a mouth. Have him watch the train all the way into the tunnel.
4. Have your baby sit on the floor with his legs apart and gently roll a ball toward him.
5. Provide wind-up toys that walk toward and away from him as he watches.

Nine Months to Eighteen Months
A. General Motor and Bilateral Development
1. Creep through, around, over, and under a family furniture obstacle course.
2. Hold your baby's hands and encourage jumping off of a small step. Try to do it over a very low object.
3. Play nursery games like Pat-a-Cake and Ten Little Indians.
4. Play games of identifying body parts.
5. Label body parts as you dress your baby.
6. Provide your baby with a kiddy-car that he has to drive around obstacles in the family room.
7. Provide him with pull toys that make sounds.
8. Allow him to climb a safe set of stairs.

B. Visual Focusing
1. Identify objects in large baby books.
2. Make up a two-piece puzzle with a circle and a square cut out. Identify each shape.
3. Provide miniature toys of different shapes and design, and label each one verbally.
4. Sort pictures of different family members. Ask your baby to identify which picture is of which family member.
5. Provide a grab-bag of objects to identify by reaching in, guessing what it is, and then pulling it out to see if he's right.

C. Visual Tracking
1. Provide a basketful of different colored clothespins to find.
2. Provide water toys that float in different directions.
3. Play ball on the floor. Occasionally use balls that have unpredictable movements.
4. Provide a toy merry-go-round. Place toy objects on it and watch them go around and fall off.

D. Eye-Hand Coordination
1. Stacking toys
2. Nesting toys
3. Blocks and pegs
4. Form boards
5. Spurt and squirt toys for the bath
6. Fillable objects and pouring toys
7. Hinges
8. Toy xylophone
9. A toy telephone

E. Binocular Coordination: Two-Eye Teaming
1. Have your baby line up large pegs in a row as if they were soldiers marching toward him or marching away.
2. When your baby is on a swing, stay in front of him and maintain eye contact.
3. Have him use a large hammer with large pegs.
4. Have your baby pour water into a container. As his skill improves, let him use containers with smaller openings.
5. Have your baby throw a ball or a beanbag onto an area on the floor or into a basket.
6. Try a balloon catch.

F. Size, Shape, Spatial Concepts
1. Try having your baby put things in order by size or length.
2. Have him put different objects in a line, and describe their positions: one, two, and three.
3. Have him place objects together that belong together, like all cups or all spoons, plates, cars, or dolls.
4. Hide an object and have him find it.
5. Have him place objects into their proper containers.
6. Scramble a stack of chips and then have your baby pick out only one type of chip. For example, have him pick out all the blue ones, although there are red and blue scattered together. Or have him pick out all the chips that look alike (for example, all the circles or all the squares).

Eighteen Months to Three Years
A. General Motor and Bilateral Development
1. Small wagon to push
2. Kiddy car
3. Push- and pull-toys
4. Screw toys

5. Incline boards of varying widths
6 Large block to use as a stepping stone
7. Wheelbarrow game: Hold the child's legs and have him walk on his hands.
8. Have your child kick a ball toward you.
9. Place a small ladder on the ground and have your child walk in between the rungs.
10. Play jumping games on a trampoline.
11. Have your child use a mixing bowl with one hand holding and the other hand mixing.

B. **Visual Focusing and Identification**
1. Find objects in a picture book or in a toy catalogue.
2. Shape puzzles with geometric shapes, animals, and community figures.
3. Match large picture cards. Hold one card about 5 feet in front of your child's face, and have him find a similar one in an array in front of him.
4. On a trip to the supermarket, let your child find objects that you are looking for. Make sure that he has a narrow field of search.

C. **Visual Tracking**
1. Large wooden beads for stringing.
2. Sort three different shapes. Place 3 cups in a horizontal row before your child. Ask your child to place buttons in the first, marbles in the second, and pegs in the third, etc.
3. Line up pegs in a horizontal row, from left to right, like soldiers.
4. Roll a large ball slowly across your child's view. Have him try to roll another ball to hit it.
5. Living room bowling: Roll a ball to knock down milk cartons.
6. Hit a stand-up punching bag.

D. **Visual-Motor Coordination (Eye-Hand, Eye-Foot, and Eye-Body)**
1. Run through and over obstacles.
2. Interlocking toys
3. Screw toys
4. Tricycle
5. Slap a floating balloon. Try to keep it from touching the ground.
6. Jigsaw puzzles of 3 to 10 pieces

7. Finger paints
8. Have your child copy a circle, and then you make it into something like a face or a balloon.
9. Modeling clay

E. **Binocular Coordination**
1. Place coins in a coin box or piggy bank.
2. Line up rows of objects.
3. Place a magnet on a string and hang it from the end of a stick. Have your child fish for metal objects.
4. Roll a ball toward your child. Have him try to trap it in the opening of a large box.
5. Help feed Daddy. Put food in Daddy's mouth.

F. **Size, Shape, and Spatial Concepts**
1. Put possessions away in the correct places.
2. Use picture books depicting things he has seen in various sizes and shapes.
3. Lincoln Log sets
4. Different-sized dolls or cars
5. String beads according to size and shape.
6. Learn to help set the table.

Three Years to Four Years

From this age on, most games stimulate an intricate combination of the necessary developing motor and visual skills (visual tracking and binocularity). The following toys and games are recommended at this stage.

- Hopping
- Stepping on shadows and cracks
- Climbing equipment
- Tricycle
- Seesaw equipment
- Bouncing board
- Rocking horse
- Wagons and wheelbarrows
- Blocks of all shapes
- Blunt scissors
- Toys with large nuts, bolts, and wrench
- Large crayons and paints
- Blowing bubbles
- Clay
- Dishes and cooking utensils

- Hand puppets
- Interlocking trains, etc.
- Beads to string
- Logs and other construction toys
- Puzzles
- Musical instruments
- Pouring and measuring toys
- Matching games
- Water play
- Sand play
- Dressing dolls and lacing toys

During this stage, it is time to aid in the development of visual memory. Toys and games for this purpose include:

- Colorform sets to build a picture with different shapes
- Mr. and Mrs. Potato Head, used to make different faces
- Match photographs to a previous vacation or place that was visited.
- Hide an object and explain where it is, and then have your child find it.
- Take an object, hide part of it, and see if your child knows what it is. If he is good at identifying it, hide more and more of it.
- Build a simple pattern with blocks. Hide it. See if he can remember and build one like it.

This is also the time to continue describing all the things and the qualities that he sees in his environment. This includes labels of sizes, of weights, of relative positions, of time sequences, etc. When you read to your child, have him point to the pictures to show you what you are reading about. This is also a good time to let him draw, fingerpaint, or sculpt the things that came from the stories you have read about. All creative expressions should be appreciated for what they are—his own inner imagery of a fertile, childlike world.

Four Years to Five Years

The following toys and games are recommended at this stage:

- Trapeze and swinging rings
- Bicycle with training wheels. (Many children this age may still prefer a tricycle.)

- Roller skates
- Cars, dump trucks, and bulldozers
- Doll carriages
- Dollhouse
- Store materials (boxes, cans, paper money, etc.)
- Beanbags and different-sized balls
- Jump rope
- Blocks
- An easel and paint
- Construction toys such as Tinker Toys and Lego
- Hand puppets
- Musical instruments (bells, drums, castanets)
- Ring toss
- Cutting and pasting materials
- A workbench with a hammer, saw, and nails
- Garden tools
- Puzzles
- Parquetry blocks
- Matching numbers and letters
- Connecting dots
- Coloring books
- Tracing within a maze
- A batting tee
- Frisbee tossing

This is the time to encourage and help foster visualization abilities. Dress-up and role-playing are excellent ways for your child to develop the ability to see and feel as if he or she were another person in another place. Provide play materials and costumes for acting out the parts of Daddy or Mommy at work or a favorite pastime, a community figure such as a fireman or policewoman, or someone you have read about or seen on a visit. Fingerpainting, drawing, sculpting, and other creative activities allow expression of the inner imagery that is dealt with.

Start off the game by asking, "What if you were——? What do you think you would do? What would you feel? What do you see?"

Other Sources for Toys and Games

An excellent book for parents is Dr. Gerald Getman's *How to Develop Your Child's Intelligence.* (See references that follow.)

REFERENCES

Belliston, Larry, and Marge Belliston. *How to Raise a More Creative Child*. Argus Communications, Allen, Texas 75002.

Bert, Kent, and Karen Calkstein. *Smart Toys for Baby from Birth to Two*. New York: Harper & Row, Colophon Books, 1981.

Getman, G.N. *How to Develop Your Child's Intelligence*. Irvine, California: Research Publications, 1984.

Gordon, Ira. *Baby Learning through Baby Play: A Parent's Guide for the First Two Years*. New York: St. Martin's Press, 1970.

Hagstrom, Julie, and Joan Morrill. *Games Babies Play*. New York: A&W Visual Library, 1979.

Karnes, Meryl B. *Small Wonder Activity Cards*. American Guidance Service, Circle Pines, Minnesota 55014.

Kavner, Richard, and Lorraine Dusky. *Total Vision*. New York: A&W Visual Library, 1978.

Levy, Dr. Janine. *The Baby Exercise Book*. New York: Pantheon Books, 1973.

Liepman, Lisa. *Your Child's Sensory World*. New York: Dial Press, 1973.

Rowley, Etta V. *Enhance Your Infant's Development*. Etta Rowley, 8133 Northeast 115th Court, Kirkland, Washington 98033.

Shakesby, Paul. *Child's Work: A Learning Guide to Joyful Play*. Philadelphia: Running Press, 1974.

Sharp, Evelyn. *Thinking Is Child's Play*. New York: Avon Books, 1970.

Sparling, Joseph, and Isabel Lewis. *Learning Games for the First Three Years*. New York: Berkley Books, 1979.

7
Living in
the Video Bubble:
Television and
the Computer

THE PSYCHOLOGY OF TELEVISION WATCHING

Television has become a potent influence in our lives. It affects our attitudes as well as the clothes that we buy. Its influence is so widespread that it even affects our choice of foods. Television was meant for entertainment, but its magic has cast a spell over our life-style. It is only recently that we have become aware of how pervasive a force it is in our lives. When we do not try to control it, we experience lethargy and inertia. This is because television is omnipresent in our lives. We cannot go anywhere without experiencing its message. It sugar-coats our dreams and drains our energies.

Television can provide entertainment and information, but for the growing mind it can also contribute to a distorted sense of reality. During the developmental years, your child will learn about the world by looking at things and events and acting upon them. In this intercourse with life's events, your child will think about what he has experienced and will respond with emotion to the results. At all times, his visual system will guide his actions and will respond to the feelings he attaches to them. This interaction between what he sees, how he acts upon it, and how he feels about what he perceives develops into the perceptual filters that guide his future behavior. In each of these real-life encounters he has responded by choice and then analyzed the results. It is this act of participation which is the key to healthy growth.

Unfortunately, this is not always the result of the experiences he has when he watches television. Television viewing is a passive situation that preselects what will be viewed, as well as when it will be viewed. It tends to distance the viewer from the experience, depressing emotions that are normally invested in what is seen. Vision is not a static act. It is a multidimensional process. Each time we look at something, the image triggers association pathways that link what we see with thoughts and words that have been previously related to that visual experience. We become aware of new possibilities for thinking, new ways of expressing an impression. We also become aware of previous sensory experiences and the feelings that were associated with what we have looked at. Along with these past and present associations, visualization of the possibilities of responding, thinking, and feeling becomes linked to the object of our attention. This is the nature of the visual process. The development of vision is a life curriculum that furnishes the situations and experiences that lead to the enrichment and dimension of our vision.

This is why it is important, especially during the critical phases of development, that children have available a varied visual menu that includes opportunities for touching, tasting, smelling, and manipulating the objects of their visual attention. They also should have the opportunity to experience the spatial and temporal dimensions of what they look at. Crucial to visual development is the opportunity to think about what is seen, as well as to share these images verbally with others. Once children have been allowed to apprehend their experiences fully, they then need time to explore them in a world of fantasy where they can imagine new possibilities for using and understanding what they have experienced. For all the benefits that TV brings us when we are unable to go out for entertainment, or when we wish to view a scene that we could not afford to travel to, it unfortunately has a great potential for limiting and perverting our visual lives. It is ironic that so sophisticated and provocative a medium is the very source of the growing visual deprivation we see in people today, especially in the so-called video children.

From the early development of a light sense in the amoeba to the sophisticated eyes of a human being, vision has always had one very basic survival purpose, and that is alerting the animal or person to events in his environment so that he will be prepared to respond for his own survival in an appropriate way. Even plants have a photo-orienting behavior: in order to survive, they turn toward light. Eyes were designed to note events in our environment and to increase our vigilance and readiness to respond to situations that require our actions. One of the unfortunate effects of television viewing is to decrease vigilance and place the viewer in a state of passivity. Some studies show that children who watch long hours of television are slower in reacting to emergency situations than are children who are engaged in other activities.

I recall one frightening Sunday morning when the snow was piling up outside the house. We had all decided to sleep late that day and then go out sledding after the snowplow had come to clear a path. At an early hour I was awakened by some unexpected noise. As I trundled out to the family room, I found one of my sons sitting on the floor, transfixed by the television screen. He would not have been aware of what was going on around him even if the house were burning down—which, unfortunately, was the case. He was surrounded by dense smoke from an electrical fire in the walls of the room. He was still somewhat in a TV daze later as he waited outside the house for the firemen to finish their job. *Television trains people not to react.* I dread the thought of what would have happened if I had slept late that snowy day.

Visual development is like weaving a very fine, intricate, and beautiful Persian carpet. The mesh is a delicate blending of experiences, thoughts, and feelings that are associated with each visual experience. Each time we look, we selectively pay attention to those things in our field which interest us. *We select what we pay attention to.* The visual experience is located in space and in time. When we look at a majestic mountain, we not only know that its beauty lies ahead of us, but we also know the physical labor required to reach it. As we behold the sight before us, many associated thoughts occur. The poetic may recall a verse from Shelley. Others may summon up various thoughts and impressions. As we survey what lies before us, we will, at some point, plan what we want to do next. For some, this may be a preparation for climbing the mountain; for others, photographing it; for still others, planning a trip home or a future visit to its top. As we look, *we are actively thinking about what we are going to do.* Each time we shift our focus, *we emotionally invest some part of ourselves.* This whole process gives our vision the multidimensional texture that it was designed to supply to our lives. Each look provides us experiences to think about and to relate to.

Mander, writing about the effects of the packaged images we are bombarded with on television, explains the flatness and dissociation of a visual experience: Looking out at a scene, "I could see the spectacular view, I knew they were spectacular. But the experience stopped at my eyes. I couldn't let it inside me. I felt nothing." "Through mere lack of exposure and practice, I had lost the ability to feel it and to tune into it or to care about it."* As we watch television, we begin to condition looking with non-involvement. We don't shift our attention. Everything to see is on that small screen. We don't shift our focus, for all the information is presented in one plane. As we continue to view passively, our emotions have become disengaged, limiting the need to alter our focus in order to examine different points of interest. *Looking at TV provides us with a flatness of experience.* This is just the opposite of the normal process of visual development and usage that is developed and has been refined since animals first acquired eyes.

If becoming a passive, uninteresting, and uninterested individual were not enough, consider the effects continued viewing has on the interaction between vision and language. Language is like a contract that binds one person to another. When we speak to each other, we convey interest by holding eye contact. We listen attentively and actively. The words we speak act as a form of currency. In effect, we trade images of our experiences. Language is the bridge these images cross from one person to another. Each image traded is agreed upon and acknowledged by other words, by exchanges of expression, or by a gesture of the listener. It is an interactive process. Each person is further enriched by this discourse. Each person further embellishes upon the image by recourse to his own past experiences, his ideas, and his thoughts. Language is not only a means to share our experiences and feelings with others, but also a means of making our feelings and impressions available to our conscious selves. There are times

*Mander, Jerry. *Four Arguments for the Elimination of Television.* New York: William Morrow, 1978.

when you feel a certain way about a situation but have no clear image of how or why. The feelings are too vague to recognize. The very struggle to put these vague sensations into words clarifies your thoughts and impressions, and an unclear mental image is then made concrete and integrated into conscious thought.

While watching television, the subliminal messages are readily absorbed by our unconscious. However, they appear to remain there as dim images, controlling our behavior but not readily accessible for conscious analysis. You have only to watch the results in people who look at television ads day after day. They frequently express a desire to go out and buy something they have seen advertised. Once they acquire the item, they exhibit pleasure in the purchase, but not necessarily in using it. Shortly after the purchase, they're anxious to acquire something else that they have seen.

Television is a potent source of stimulation for the unconscious. Dreams and fantasies are aroused, but conscious thinking is depressed. The very process of analyzing and looking beneath the surface experience to understand our feelings and motives requires a degree of vigilance and involvement that develops over time. It is supported by an active visual system. The visual system is always alert, moving, scanning, focusing. Eyes are the major source of contact with the world. Their very activity encourages and enhances mental activity and alertness. As we watch television—especially after two or three hours—we habituate to the light stimulus. The brain alters its active functions. The center for logic and analysis becomes quiet, while that part of the brain that we associate with a lack of definition, with inactivity and physical inertia, begins to take over. It is a state of uncritical acceptance.

There has never been a more effective means of controlling people's thoughts and actions than television. It provides the mechanism for physiologically putting people into an uncritical, receptive state. The only thing necessary is then to supply the message. That's what advertising is all about. Every time you walk down the street or go into a store, note how many people purchase what is currently being advertised on television. Imagine the potential use of television by politicians and other people who seek influence and power.

Besides arousing the desire to purchase or acquire something, television is good at entertaining us, especially if little action or thought is required. I have been impressed with those television programs that have whetted my children's appetite for more knowledge about a subject. However, I have been very disappointed when they have not been able to follow through and read for themselves. There have been times that I have read them a story that they have seen on television. They professed an anxiousness to have the story read to them. But reading and television are not the same. Most of the time, television packages the images in small time sequences. This discourages the sustained attention necessary for reading and other tasks requiring concentration. The encouraged passivity that occurs while watching television does not lend itself to thinking about what you are witnessing. There is very little probing below the surface. One image is presented after another. You absorb what you see and then watch the next scene. There is no stopping to think or going back to check. There is no desire to question what went on before and how it relates to what you are seeing now. Is it any wonder that we see students today who have not developed critical thinking or problem-solving skills? They do not want to take the time and mental effort to evaluate their experience. The result is that they live primarily on the surface of a sensory experience. They are not able to put that experience in context and have difficulty sorting out what is important or relevant.

When we read, we not only acquire information, but also develop thinking skills. Reading is an active process that requires us to think about what we are reading. There are levels of critical reading and thinking. Not all readers critically think about what they have read. Some uncritically accept whatever the author has written. However, the reading process lends itself to developing these critical skills. The pace of reading, rereading, and stopping to think is set by the reader, according to his needs, his desires, and the level of difficulty of the material. It is an active process in which the reader consciously attends. There is an increased level of brain activity, which indicates that thoughts are consciously being processed. It is not unusual for a reader to take time to mull over what he has read and relate it to what he has experienced or read before. This whole process reminds me of the act of striving that you see when watching someone involved in growing.

The opposite is true of the people I see in my practice who have reading problems—both children and adults. Their involvement in reading is a passive one. They read as if expecting the thoughts and ideas will be predigested for them. Some are in the same passive state that is common among television viewers. They have their eyes open, but they have disengaged their active mind from what they are viewing.

Did you ever try to discuss a television program with your children? It goes something like this:

"What was the story about?"

"It was gross."

"What happened in the story?"

"Well, this car crashed into a restaurant and killed a little girl."

"Who was in the story?"

"A policeman who got shot."

The lack of detail and context with thoughts out of sequence is maddening. This is especially true if you get to see the program and it is a story about a bank robbery. As the robbers hold up a bank, they shoot a security guard who tries to stop them. What follows is a hurly-burly chase scene that ends up with the getaway car going out of control and crashing into a restaurant window, killing a little girl.

Is it any wonder that 25 percent of the adults in our country are not able to address a letter properly? They cannot read well enough to protect their rights when they purchase something. We may have a low rate of illiteracy, but practical literacy is something else. As an invention, television is marvelous. As an influence upon our ability to be active, independent, and lead a more fully enriched life, it leaves a lot to be desired.

The Television Malaise

1. Average family watches 6½ hours a day.
2. Children average 4 hours a day.
3. Over one million children are watching TV at midnight.

DANGER SIGNS

1. Television is not watched as a family.
2. Television disrupts family mealtimes.
3. Television watching has replaced family conversation.
4. Children put on the television as soon as they come home from school.
5. Saturday morning is spent in front of the TV set.

6. Children are bored when they can't watch television.
7. Television is chosen over other activities.
8. The television set has preempted play space and play time.
9. Children can't write simple stories or organize their thoughts for a letter to a family member.
10. The child is watching television for more than twelve hours a week on a regular basis.

SUGGESTIONS FOR HEALTHY GROWTH EXPERIENCES

1. Limit television viewing to two hours or less, five days a week.
2. Help your child to choose a TV program.
3. Make television viewing a shared experience.
4. Discuss what was seen.
5. Critically discuss what does not represent a real life experience. This is especially true of sit-coms and advertisements.
6. Make sure that your child has a chance to develop other sources of entertainment and relaxation.
   Parents are powerful role models, so this applies equally to the parents.
7. Provide a place and plenty of opportunities to explore creative activities—arts and crafts, construction materials, etc.
8. Have your child discuss a program you both have seen and then let him write a story about it.
9. In our family we have instituted a story time right before dinner. Sometimes Dad reads a story and then the family discusses it at dinner and sometimes the reading is shared with the children.
10. Whenever possible, have your children read a story about the events displayed on television.

VIEWING DISTANCE AND LIGHTING

1. The approximate distance that television should be watched is between four and five times the diameter of the set.
   If the set is a 12-inch set, then the viewing distance is between four and five feet.
   It should never be less than two feet.
   If you have a very small screen, get a magnifier or else throw it out.
2. Always view the screen from a straight ahead position.

3. Never view television in a pitch-dark room.
4. The surrounding light should be about half the brightness needed for reading.
5. No area within sight of the viewer should be brighter than the screen itself.

Average reading, studying and sewing requires 30 to 70 foot-candles.

For ease in figuring, consider that a lamp with a diffusing element under a shade will give the following light levels.

60 watt light bulb	15 foot-candles
100 " " "	35 " "
150 " " "	45 " "
200 " " "	75 " "

VIDEO DISPLAY TERMINALS

Another aspect of the video revolution is just now becoming ubiquitous in our lives. The computer with its video display terminal (VDT) can now be seen wherever you go. You see it in stores, at places of business, and now more and more in homes and schools. And along with this proliferation of VDTs has come a proliferation of health complaints—so many that the National Institute for Occupational Safety and Health carried out a series of studies to determine the nature of the problem. A survey of operators who use VDTs reported significantly more discomfort among these users than with people who work with printed material only. Eighty-four percent of video terminal users reported generalized eyestrain. Sixty-seven percent reported a burning sensation of their eyes, and 40 percent reported that their vision had become blurred after using a video terminal. There are other reports of color vision changes and possible cataracts and glaucoma, as well as physical, mental, and psychological disturbances.

The problems that arise when using a computer and VDT appear to be related to several factors. The first factor is the work-station itself and the posture required to comfortably support the task. The ideal posture can be seen in the following drawing.

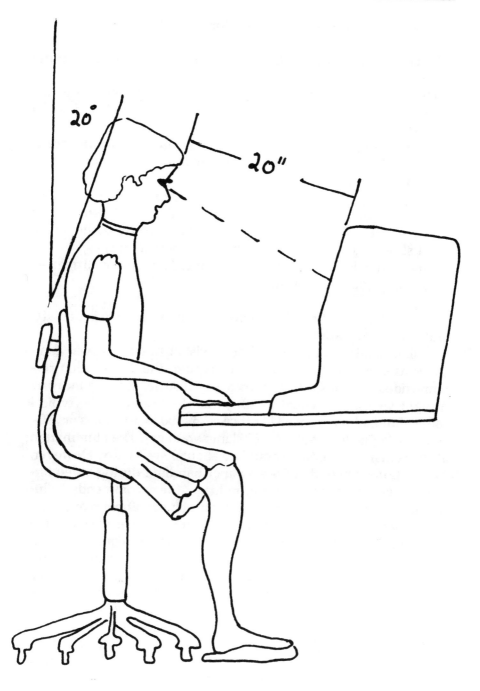

Ideal Posture for Video Viewing.

The ideal workstation allows for the following:

- Screen, copy, and console are all at the same distance from the user's eyes.
- The user's trunk should be straight, slightly inclined forward, about 20 degrees from the hips, with eyes directed 20 degrees down.
- The user's upper arm should be vertical, in line with the body, and the lower arm should be horizontal, or slightly lower than the horizontal.
- The viewing distance to the manuscript, to the screen, and to the keyboard should be constant at about 45 to 50 centimeters (about 18 to 20 inches). The screen can be slightly farther away but should not exceed 70 centimeters (about 28 inches).
- Any head twisting to view material should not exceed 30 degrees from the spinal axis of the body.

Constant postural deviations can cause fatigue, irritability, and visual adaptation.

Illumination is important for all visual situations even computer use. When one is reading or typing, the illumination recommended is from 750 to approximately 1600 lux. Lux is a measure of light levels. It is equal to 10 × one foot-candle. The typical room illumination of a well lit office is 75–100 foot-candles or 750–1000 lux (equal to about 200–250 lamp wattage). The illumination at the actual workstation should be about 500–700 lux. However, in situations where there is no paper handling during video terminal viewing, such as in the military, the recommended illumination can be as low as 50 lux. Because most offices require the user to go constantly from screen viewing to paper viewing, the computer in the usual business office or school requires a great deal of visual compromising. In a normal office situation, the light in the room may be too bright for comfortable video terminal viewing. The greater the overall illumination, the greater the chance that there will be reflective glare from the set. Offices have to eliminate this problem by dramatically reducing the illumination at the video terminal workstation. Unfortunately, they have kept the surrounding areas—within the visual field—at the same high light levels. The result is turmoil to the visual system. The video terminal operator finds that he is constantly readjusting his eyes for the change in contrast. This requires large shifts in the photochemical response of the retina. The body's stores of vitamin A become quickly depressed. Along with this change is the required muscular effort to continuously readjust the pupil. Just imagine waking up in the dead of night and turning on your nightlight and then shutting it off. Now imagine doing this one thousand times in succession. Not only would you develop eye symptoms, but you would also become quite irritable. Until further research gives us better answers, I have developed the following illumination guidelines for the video terminal workstation.

1. Proper illumination for computer viewing should be 250–500 lux or 25–50 foot-candles.
2. Computer illumination should be at or slightly below the illumination of the paper (equal to 100–150 watt bulb).
3. To avoid the problem of reflected glare, make sure that the illumination falling on the screen when it is not being used is at most one-half that of the illumination it receives when it is used. If the illumination falling on the screen when it is off is as high as when it is on, then there will be too much reflected glare for comfortable viewing.
4. The brightness of the video characters should be about 10 times that of the background.
5. The visual field that surrounds the screen, or approximately 2 feet on each side of the screen, should not be more than 3 times the brightness of the screen when it is on for use. Ideally, there should be a graduated change in illumination as the eye shifts from screen to work paper to surrounding background.
6. There should be no bright sources that reflect from the screen into the viewer's eyes. This can come from an overhead light fixture or from an uncurtained window. A good way to determine whether there is any reflected image that will cause difficulty is the mirror test. While seated in a viewing position, have another person move a small mirror over the entire face of the video screen. Watch the mirror for bright images. They can sometimes come from surprising sources, such as a bright dress or sunlight peeking through the window.

You can use a camera exposure meter to roughly estimate the illumination at a workstation with the following procedure.

1. Set the camera's exposure meter at ASA 100.
2. Set the camera's shutter speed at $\frac{1}{25}$ second, or the closest setting.

3. Place a piece of paper with written material on it next to the video terminal in its usual place. Adjust the illumination on the paper until your exposure meter reads F5.6, or the closest setting.

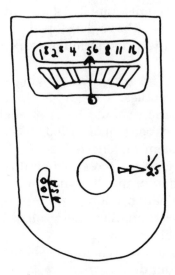

4. Next, read the exposure of your video screen when it has material displayed on it. Adjust the brightness until the exposure meter in your camera reads F4.

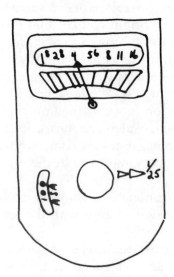

5. Next, take an exposure reading of the surrounding 4 feet—at least 2 feet on each side of the screen. The exposure reading for the surrounding view should be approximately F8, not less.

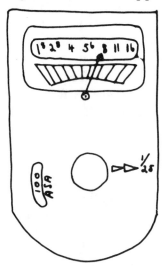

6. Turn the screen off and take an exposure reading of the blank screen. The exposure reading should be F2 or less. The closer it is to the original F4, the greater the possibility of too high a level of reflected glare. (Note: Keep in mind that each F-stop change is twice the amount of light as you go to lower numbers. For example, F4 to F2.8 is twice the light. When the exposure meter moves up the scale—for example, F4 to F5.6—you are recording half the amount of light.)

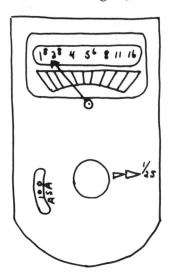

Some video terminal users have good illumination but still experience discomfort. The discomfort may be the result of screen flicker that disrupts their binocular responses. For characters to become visible on the video screen, phosphorus has to be placed on the insert of the screen and then electrically activated. The activation occurs at a fixed rate. Sometimes, however, the rate is too slow for the viewer's visual system. The result then is a flicker that is seen in the periphery of vision. This on-and-off regeneration of characters may interfere with comfortable viewing. This is especially true of people who have binocular visual problems.

One way to determine if this is happening to your set is to view a corner of the set. Out of the corner of your eye, note whether the center of the set has any flicker of its images. If it does, the recharging rate may not be appropriate for the viewer's eyes. The use of tints has sometimes proved beneficial for some people who have this problem. Another aspect that must be looked at is the size of the letters and their spacing. For comfortable viewing at 50 centimeters (about 20 inches) the vertical height of a lowercase *o* should be between 2 and 4 millimeters, and the spacing should be approximately one-half times the vertical height. If the letters are smaller than this size, or the spacing smaller, loss of information and eyestrain can result. The spacing between lines should be 1–1½ times the vertical height of the *o*.

In the coming years, more and more children will be using video terminals at school and at home. This is the time to instill good working habits and adequate preventive knowledge. Make sure your child follows these guidelines:

1. If any of the following symptoms are noted after your child uses a video terminal, discontinue its use and take him or her to an optometrist.
   Headaches
   Blurred vision
   Eye irritation
   Slowed adjustment of the focusing mechanism when shifting attention from one place to another
   Any noticeable change in color vision
   Double vision
   Difficulty adjusting eyes to different light contrasts
   Redness of eye tissues
   Blinking or rubbing of eyes

Spots or the sensation of floating substances
Upper neck or shoulder discomfort
General fatigue
Irritability
Increase in errors in noting what is seen
Facial twitch
Sensation of seeing cobwebs or dull areas in the visual field

2. Have your optometrist evaluate your child's vision at the 20-inch distance to see if any protective lenses would be useful.

3. Make sure that your child takes a visual break every twenty minutes or so. Have him stand up and move around. Make sure he shifts his eyes off the screen and looks at other distances.

4. Follow the guidelines on lighting. The screen characters should be 10 times brighter than the screen background. Reading material should be properly illuminated. The screen illumination should be slightly less than the illumination on the paper being read. There should be no reflected glare from screen. The surrounding illumination should not exceed 3 times the level of the screen illumination when it is on for use.

5. Make sure that the screen is regularly cleaned and the set is in proper focus.

6. Follow the guidelines on posture and placement of the set. The screen and the keyboard should be about 45 to 50 centimeters (18 to 20 inches) away. The child's trunk should be straight. He should be inclined from his hips, approximately 20 degrees. His upper arm should be vertical, in line with his body, and the lower arm should be held approximately horizontal. Any head twists should not exceed 30 degrees when viewing material.

Computers are here to stay. They can provide children with many hours of amusement, entertainment, and information. However, let's be sure that they are protected from the abuse that video terminals can sometimes inflict.

8
Vision in Competitive Play and Team Sports

"Suddenly, as if a light had blinked on in my mind, I remembered and began to understand some puzzling childhood problems. Reading had literally given me headaches as a teenager. But two doctors had each given me a clean bill of health. My father accused me of just trying to duck my homework. I studiously avoided ball sports, attributing this to my distaste for teamwork, not to my inability to catch a pass or to shoot baskets in the gym."

How often have I heard similar stories from the adults I have examined. Play is very important in a child's development. Early play allows children the opportunity to learn about themselves and how to deal with their environment. Later, group play with peers requires that children learn how to submerge their identity as individuals and find gratification by becoming a part of the group. It is preparation for becoming part of the adult work world. Children who are unsure of themselves feel threatened when they are required to participate in group activities. They either withdraw from the group activity or try to protect themselves by bullying their way into a leadership position. Unfortunately, the leadership role that they take on is often for purposes of self-gratification rather than as a means of finding the common goal necessary to satisfy the group's needs. We often relate this type of growth pattern to the lack of an early affective interchange which interferes with the child's developing a sense of confidence about himself in a play situation. It is frustrating for a child to be told by adults that he is stupid or clumsy, or that he surely will be unsuccessful in his attempts. The adult-child relationship during play should center on sharing the fun of growing and learning. It is not only the means of a child's developing a sense of himself and his competence during participation, but also the vehicle for establishing a lifetime relationship of easy communication and sharing between child and parent.

Although many of us recognize this need for support and early socialization, few adults recognize the importance that visual skills have in allowing us to participate successfully in sports and group games. I remember the first time I saw little Clyde. His sad face was sure to provoke sympathy from anyone who looked at him. Clyde's mother had brought him in for examination that January morning because he was not holding his own at school. But that was not what was troubling little Clyde. In the car, Clyde and his mother had been discussing summer camps that he might attend. Clyde was unhappy because all the camps his parents had visited emphasized competition and team sports. During the examination, his sad story came out. He told me he didn't like team sports because he was never any good. He always ran the wrong way or fumbled the ball. If he wasn't the last one picked, it was because the other kids were still fighting to see who would be stuck with him. Clyde said that, unfortunately, he liked "girls' sports," such as gymnastics and swimming.

Clyde didn't realize two things. First, the sports he liked were not necessarily reserved for girls, but simply emphasized individual performance, not teamwork. Second, he didn't realize that his eyes mixed him up when he was playing. This was also the reason he was struggling in school. Clyde had difficulty tracking a ball with his eyes. He would frequently lose it in midspace. The same thing happened when he read. He would lose his place on the line. Clyde also had an eye-teaming problem. He seemed to judge things to be farther away than they actually were. As a result, he would swing late or else, when he went to catch the ball, he would reach out to it too late. Before he knew it, the ball hit him in the head. This binocular problem interfered with his ability to understand spatial concepts and to concentrate when he was reading.

After I demonstrated to Clyde why he was having trouble, I saw a little smile peek out, and then it was masked by a concerned and skeptical look. It was almost as if he were saying, "Can I really believe this guy?" Clyde participated in a vision therapy program that winter until he left for camp. The next time I saw him was the following September. He came strutting in as if he owned the office. When I asked him about his summer, he proudly told me about the home run that he hit that had won an important game. Then he added, "But I'm pretty good at baseball. My counselor told me that I was one of the best hitters at camp."

What Clyde and his parents had learned was that Clyde was not a clumsy, daydreaming kid. Clyde had chosen the sports that he could participate in because they didn't demand the very visual skills that he had not yet developed.

When something like that happens, a child has several choices. First, he can withdraw from all athletic performance. Second, he can select only those sports that do not require the visual skills that he has not yet developed. This is almost always an unconscious decision, for few children or adults recognize that they like certain activities because they have the necessary visual skills for that activity. The third choice is usually taken by children who are (or who feel they are) being pressured to excel at a particular sport. The lack of visual skill makes it difficult, but not impossible. We can then see a child or an adult work hard to compensate. They may even excel, but if you look carefully, you will see the telltale signs of a visual problem:

• Inconsistent performance
• Skilled performance only in specific aspects of the game
• Decreasing performance as the pressure increases
• Decreasing performance when tired or troubled by outside influences
• Inability to attend skillfully to more than one activity at a time
• Discomfort during or after a game that is not related to the muscles used
• Skilled performance only when the body is stationary or in balance, and not when moving or out of balance

Some children even grow up to become highly paid professional athletes, but they still do not recognize that their lack of efficient visual abilities limits their skillful performance. I have seen some professionals whose performance deteriorates under certain circumstances—for example, the baseball player who is not able to coordinate a bunt with a steal from first base, or the tennis player who complains that she's not able to play in the late afternoon when the shadows begin to encroach upon the court. Many superstars are just beginning to understand the relationship between successful performance and visual skills. Barbara Potter, the 1982 U.S. indoor tennis champion, has said, "When I'm playing really well I just feel like the ball becomes larger and I see it better." Baseball's Pete Rose recently attested to the importance he places on his visual abilities. He said, "Other players worry about when their legs will go. I've always been more concerned about my eyes." Many people I have spoken to agree that their eyes are an important part of their ability to compete successfully. But most people think only about their ability to see clearly. They're totally unaware of the other visual skills that play an important role in guiding athletic performance.

In the last ten years, many people have become a part of the fitness revolution, and there has been a boom in participation in all sports. As a result, some high school, college, and professional teams have taken on optometrists as vision consultants. Their work, which has resulted in a better understanding of the underlying visual needs in different sports, is only now slowly filtering down to the general practitioner in optometry. I feel that it is very important for parents to know more about the relationship between visual fitness and successful sports participation. This is especially true while their children are growing and depending on those very skills. As soon as children interact, they like to compete. They feel good and have a sense of enjoyment about their competitive accomplishments. But when a child goes up at bat and misses, or out to catch a pass and drops it, he doesn't blame his visual ability, he blames himself. He begins to think of himself as a clumsy person. That image can persist throughout his life. The time to correct it is before it starts.

VISUAL SKILLS FOR SPORTS

There is no question that seeing clearly is important in many sports. Ninety-eight percent of athletes have 20/20 acuity or better. But there are other visual skills that also play an important role in supporting successful participation. When you have your child's vision evaluated, make sure that the following skills are also investigated.

Dynamic Visual Acuity

Dynamic visual acuity is the ability to see clearly when in motion. It enables a player to move his eyes rather than his head or body when the ball is in play. It also allows a child to see the ball as soon as it leaves his opponent's racket and to quickly know where it is going and when it will get there. If your child plays hockey, it will allow him to follow the puck, especially when he's in motion. It allows for following the action, when on the move, with the eyes instead of with the body. The result of the ability to freely move the eyes instead of the body will be less strain in maintaining body balance and on the nervous system.

Peripheral Vision

Peripheral vision is the ability to see out of the corners of the eyes while concentrating on a task. It allows your child, on the soccer field, to move the ball down the field, to know where his teammates are, and to know where the opponents are. Peripheral vision acts as a guidance system that helps orient the body and eyes to the task. It is necessary if your child is to avoid crashing into walls or fences while chasing fly balls. It also helps to guide the player to the field boundaries. Many vision specialists believe that this is one of the visual skills that allowed O.J. Simpson to run so skillfully while eluding opponents who were swerving in from the sides to tackle him. If you take your child skiing, make sure that his peripheral vision is well developed so that he can navigate the slope while keeping track of the traffic.

Depth Perception

The ability to judge distances between oneself and the ball, opponents, and teammates depends on cooperation between the two eyes. When both eyes do not work coordinately, the ball can be perceived to be in a different place rather than in its actual location. Some children swing too early and blame it on impatience, but in reality it is because they perceive the ball to be closer than it actually is. Depth perception also allows your child to avoid colliding with other players. It is a necessary skill that aids in determining when to reach to catch, how hard to throw a ball to make it reach its proper destination, and when and how hard to swing in order to connect with the ball. Swimmers need good depth perception when approaching turns or timing their break for the finish line.

Visual Tracking Ability

Tracking is the ability to follow a moving object smoothly with the eyes. Its importance is felt in all sports, from soccer or basketball to tossing a Frisbee. It also involves the ability to shift visual attention from one object to another. As a football player goes out for a pass, he watches it leave the quarterback's hands. At this point he begins to judge where he is going and how fast he has to run to get there. He continues to track the ball into his hands. At that point, he releases his visual attention from the ball and looks to where he is going next. If he does not track the ball into his hands, he risks dropping it. If he releases attention too late, he winds up at the bottom of a pile of opponents.

Eye–Hand-Foot-Body Coordination

The ability to integrate what the eyes see with what the body does allows a player to be in the right place at the right time. It allows him to score consistent baskets, make faster turns in the water, and kick a soccer ball while maintaining balance. In horse-back riding, it is crucial that eye-body skills be well developed. The position of the rider's head will affect the horse's balance. Adjusting the horse's stride when approaching a fence requires an instantaneous body response to what is seen. Eye-body skills are also necessary for skating around a rink and for diving.

Visualization Skills

Visualization is the ability to see a situation or action with your mind's eye before you're actually involved. It is the ability to sense tacklers that you could not possibly see. It is an ability to mentally practice a perfect serve moments before tossing the ball into the air. Most good gymnasts and dancers will practice the movements in their mind's eye before they perform. Visualization means knowing where the basket is without looking at it, or where the goal is while taking a ball downfield. Practicing visualizing a perfect response will allow the body to automatically perform. Many professional golfers have learned to visualize a perfect stroke and then let the body execute it.

Visual Reaction Time

Visual reaction time is the ability to quickly identify what and where an object is so that a rapid response can be made to it. As you speed up your ability to identify objects moving in space, they appear to move more slowly and appear to be larger. Rod Carew, on a hitting streak, said, "Every pitch looks like a grapefruit." The faster you can understand what you are looking at, the more time you will have to act.

If your child wants to become a serious athlete, I would suggest that you contact the Sports Vision Section of the American Optometric Association, 243 North Lindbergh Boulevard, St. Louis, Missouri 63141. Ask for a list of behavioral optometrists who specialize in sports vision.

PROTECTION

The revolution in physical fitness that has swept the United States has provided some very significant health benefits to those who have participated. Unfortunately, along with the benefits, we have seen an increasing rate of injuries. A recent 1983 study indicated that there are more than 100,000 eye injuries each year. The five- to fourteen-year-old age group has the largest number of injuries in baseball, football, bicycling, and soccer. To me, this is an unacceptable rate of injury. Today we are seeing more and more children participating in league play. I feel that there are pluses and minuses to participating in controlled, competitive athletics for children. The positive side is that it provides a healthy outlet for energies while they learn fair play, good sportsmanship, and the rules of the game. This is especially true when we find that children in the United States today are more overweight and in poorer condition than they were in the past. Sports should provide an awareness of hygiene, diet, rest, exercise, as well as sport and game orientation. It should promote a willingness to take responsibility for lifelong fitness. The negative side of league play is when children take themselves too seriously. An overemphasis on winning robs the game of joy. It also short-circuits the necessary warm-up and cool-down periods that are necessary for protection against injury. As a result, too many children push themselves in this situation to the point of injury. Soccer is an example of this. It is one of the fastest-growing children's sports around today. When we look at the years from 1973 to 1978, we find that eye injuries increased by 58 percent in all sports. But if we look at soccer alone, we find that the rate is 260 percent, and one-third of these injuries were in children between the ages of five and fourteen. We want children to play, but we do not want them to get hurt. Anyone who participates in a sport where there is a chance of eye injury should wear an eye-protector. This is especially true in racket sports, ice hockey, football, and soccer. If protective glasses are worn, make sure that the frames are of industrial strength or that they are sport-type eyeguards with cushion supports, and that they are fitted with impact-resistant, polycarbonate safety lenses. Also, I would recommend the following guidelines, established by the American Alliance for Health, Physical Education, and Recreation and Dance, when you consider having your child participate in organized sports.

Age six: Noncontact sports that require individual skills are appropriate. Examples are swimming, gymnastics, track and field, tennis, and skating.

Age eight: Team sports that require individual skills are appropriate. Examples are basketball, volleyball, soccer, and wrestling.

Ages ten to twelve: Contact sports are appropriate. These include rugby, football, and hockey. The name of the game is fun and a growing sense of competence. Winning should not be the only thing.

9
Eating Right for Sight

When I went to school, my course on nutrition included the comment, "All you have to do is eat three balanced meals a day, and then you will have nothing to worry about." Unfortunately, there are still practitioners who do not realize the limitations of that philosophy.

I once examined a young woman who complained of a burning sensation in her eyes. Her eyelids were frequently red and had small crusts on them. When she had to read at school, she experienced occasional blurring of her vision and sensitivity to light as she continued to push herself during reading tasks. These symptoms had been steadily getting worse for the last six months. She had no other symptoms except a mild lethargy. The last six months had been relatively quiet ones in her life. She had no major illnesses, and she had led a rather sedentary life, sitting around the house after school most of the time. She had also told me that she had gained about twelve pounds in that period. My examination did not reveal any gross ocular abnormalities, although the whites of her eyes did appear to be slightly red. Her functional visual skills (eye tracking, focusing, and eye teaming) were very sluggish. She had also begun to develop some nearsightedness. Because of the general and ocular sluggishness, the recent weight gain, and the beginning nearsightedness, I felt that endrocrinological and nutritional evaluations were necessary before attempting to do anything visually. The results of the laboratory report indicated that she had an underactive thyroid and was depleted in vitamins A, B_1, B_2, B_3, B_6, and B_{12}, folic acid, chromium, and zinc. It also appeared that she had an excessive amount of lead in her system. As a result of the laboratory tests, she changed her nutritional habits and began a program of active physical exercise. The only vision therapy she was given at the time was some simple eye focusing procedures. After approximately three months, she returned for a reevaluation. She looked terrific. Her change in diet and her exercise program helped her to look and feel better. She had lost about ten pounds. But what surprised and delighted me most were the very significant visual changes that showed up on her new examination. At the initial examination, her visual acuity was recorded as 20/30 for each eye. Now her acuity was 20/20 for each eye, and there was no measurable nearsightedness, just a small amount of normal farsightedness. Also, the focusing sluggishness was gone. I felt, because of these findings, that no further therapy was necessary.

The story sounds amazing, but it is absolutely true. I only wish that more visual problems were so readily treatable.

The brain and the eye comprise less than 2 percent of the total body weight. Yet they require approximately 25 percent of the body's nutrition. It only takes about sixty seconds to starve the eye of nutrition, and then it begins to get permanent damage. On the other hand, the body's musculature can go for up to five minutes without any nutrition before sustaining damage.

Eyes can function beautifully, but not without the necessary nutrients to fuel their actions. Why is that so difficult if all we have to do is eat three good meals? Well, that may have been true a thousand years ago when our choices were simpler. At that time, patterns of growing, gathering, and cooking food were handed down for generations. What worked to keep people healthy was kept in the diet; what made people sick was discarded. Today things are no longer so simple. We live in a world where many subtle and not-so-subtle influences affect what we eat and how it is absorbed. These changes include the medications that we take, the changed soil that foods are grown in, the processing of the foods we eat, the presence of various additives in prepared foods, and the improper, nutrition-destroying methods of preparing foods. The foods we eat today do not always serve our needs as they should. This chapter is not intended as a complete course on nutrition, but when accepted medical authorities casually accept the fact that a high percentage of people in the United States have deficiencies in things such as iron, B vitamins, zinc, and chromium, it is time to look more critically at how and what we eat, and how that affects our vision. For those who want to further their knowledge in the area of nurition, I have included a list of recommended books in the bibliography.

What we eat affects our overall health, our thinking and our vision, as well as our mood, awareness, and alertness. Our nutrition helps to build cells which are the building blocks of our muscles and organs. Only when these are healthy can we expect to be able to perform adequately. If, on the other hand, our diets are saturated with sugars, refined white flour, salt, artificial flavoring, and preservatives, and we are not careful to alter our nutrition to meet the needs of stress situations that we encounter, infections that we have, and side effects of medications that we take, then we will eventually have unhealthy changes in the fluids and tissues of our bodies. Slowly, these changes will show up in our movements, learning ability, perceptions, and reactions to our environment. As an example, animal studies using the food additive Red Dye No. 3 have shown that ingestion of the dye can result in hyperactive responses in a fluorescent-lighted environment. Possibly the same thing may be occurring in classrooms with hyperactive children who have learning disabilities.

The essential ingredients that all of us—adults and children—need are water, oxygen, fatty acids, proteins (amino acids), minerals (which are enzyme activators), carbohydrates, and vitamins (which are co-enzyme factors). These are needed in the proper balance, and they must be readily available for absorption and usage. It is when we are missing one of these essential ingredients or they are not in proper balance that we begin to have difficulty.

The general causes of nutritional problems are the following:

1. The foods we eat may not have a full complement of the vitamins and minerals we need because of the way they were processed or because they were grown in deficient soil.

2. Nutrients in foods may have been lost because of long and improper storage, improper methods of cooking or preparation, or exposure to light or air.
3. The body may not be able to properly digest or absorb necessary nutrients. This can be due to organ malfunction, genetic interference, or medication. For example, children who regularly use cough syrup containing alcohol lose B vitamins, iron, magnesium, and zinc.
4. We can lose nutrients because of chronic diarrhea or conditions such as peptic ulcer and colitis.
5. The nutrients we take in can be lost if we use caffeine (as in coffee, tea, or cola drinks), nicotine, sugar, refined flour, and preservatives.
6. Nutrients are rapidly used up when we are under stress, thus creating a demand for replenishment which our diet may be inadequate to supply.
7. A deficiency in certain nutrients may make it impossible for the body to utilize even those nutrients that are in the diet. This is because some nutrients work best when they're taken with certain other nutrients. For example, calcium requires vitamin D for proper absorption. Our needs for essential amino acids may not be satisfied unless some proteins are taken along with a complementary protein. This is especially true for vegetable proteins. For example, legumes would be complete if eaten with whole-grain rice, wheat, or corn or with milk or cheese. Grains would form a complete protein if eaten together with legumes or milk products, and so on.

Good nutrition for your child means more than giving him a few vitamins. Good nutrition is becoming aware of what foods your child eats and what nutrients he is supplied with. Nutrition is very important to the orderly development of your child. While this is especially true in the very early years, when malnutrition can actually result in stunted brain growth, it will be true throughout his growing years when he is learning to use his body and mind. Inadequate nutrition interferes with his ability to integrate and act on the things he sees. The results can seriously interfere with overall development. It is important for a child to establish good eating habits early in life. The earlier he becomes accustomed to eating properly, the easier it is for him to maintain those habits throughout his life. In order to ensure that his total food intake is divided into the proper proportions of protein, carbohydrates, and fats, it is desirable to establish, from an early age, a varied menu. Each week should allow for meals composed of each of three food groups—proteins, carbohydrates, and fats. Your child's menu should also contain foods that are rich in vitamins and minerals. Salads, fresh fruits, and fresh vegetables should be a part of every day's meals. All foods, including fats, sugars, and starches, are important. The secret is in having a balance of all the necessary nutrients: proteins, carbohydrates, fats, vitamins, and minerals.

Essential Nutrients, Vitamins, and Minerals

PROTEIN

What is it?
Your body is made up of protein. Proteins are composed of up to twenty-two amino acids, of which eight to ten cannot be synthesized by the body and so must be supplied to it on a daily basis. A protein containing all of the essential amino acids in generous amounts is said to be complete. Proteins lacking any of these essential amino acids are considered incomplete. Body tissue cannot be built of incomplete protein. Two or more incomplete proteins must be combined so that each furnishes the amino acids lacking in the other.

What is it used for?
Every body part contains protein. All growth, development, and maintenance of health and life itself are dependent upon an adequate supply of complete proteins. No living being survives without protein. The word itself means "of first importance."

How do we obtain it?
There are two kinds of proteins: those from animal and those from plant sources. In general, animal proteins (meat, milk, milk products such as cheese and yogurt, fish, fowl, and eggs) are complete, while those from plant sources are generally incomplete and must be combined with complementary foods to become complete. (Wheat germ, brewer's yeast, and soybeans are exceptions to this rule and are complete protein sources.)

Combinations to form complete proteins
Whole grains should be combined with milk products or eggs or legumes. Legumes should be combined with milk products or eggs or grains. Nuts and seeds should be combined with milk products or eggs to form complete proteins.

How much do we need?
There is no exact amount that is universally agreed upon. However, the general recommendation is 2 grams for every 2.2 pounds of body weight for a growing child, and 1 gram for every 2.2 pounds of body weight for an adult. An extra amount of protein is needed for pregnant or nursing women, babies, or anyone ill or recovering from an illness or under any special physical or other stress.

Protein content (in grams) of some common foods*

1	egg	6 gm
1	qt. milk (whole, skim, or buttermilk)	32–35 gm
½	lb. meat, fish, or fowl	15–22 gm
½	cup cooked soybeans	20 gm
½	cup cottage cheese	20 gm
2	slices American or Swiss cheese	10 gm
½	cup brewer's yeast powder	24 gm
½	cup wheat germ	24 gm

*Source: Wynder, Ernst. *The Book of Health*. Franklin Watts, N.Y.: The American Health Foundation, 1981.

What are the signs of deficiency?

Pregnant women who eat inadequate amounts of protein frequently give birth to mentally retarded babies. If, during the first four years, a child's diet is deficient in protein, there tends to be a decreased number of brain cells, and those brain cells tend to exhibit numerous abnormalities. Prolonged deficiency of protein can cause anemia, kidney disease, liver disease, peptic ulcer, poor wound healing, lack of resistance to infections, irritability, fatigue, mental retardation in children, poor vision, weakness, wasting, and numerous other maladies.

CARBOHYDRATES

What are they?

Carbohydrates include various compounds produced by plants in the form of sugars or starches.

What are they used for?

A moderate amount of carbohydrates is essential to a child's metabolic process. They provide energy and assist in digestion and assimilation. They break down inside cells to release energy. The primary source of the brain's energy is the sugar glucose, which is obtained mainly from starch in the diet.

How do we obtain them?

There are two kinds of carbohydrates: simple (or refined) and complex. As a general rule, the simple and refined sources should be kept to a minimum, and you should try to introduce as many complex carbohydrates into your child's diet as possible. Some sources of complex carbohydrates are whole grains (and whole grain cereals, pastas, flours, and bread), brown rice, vegetables and fruits, fresh fruit or vegetable juice, corn, and legumes.

How much do we need?

Most children require about 1 gram of carbohydrate daily for every 3 pounds of body weight.

What are the signs of deficiency?

One sign of deficiency is cloudiness in ocular tissues.

HYDROCARBONS: FATS AND OILS

What are they?
All fats are made up of fatty acids. Those acids are either saturated or unsaturated. Fats that are usually solid at room temperature are called *saturated*. They are found in meats and coconut. They can increase cholesterol, which is essential for conversion of sunlight into vitamin D in the skin. Cholesterol is also needed for normal liver function and is absolutely necessary for the production of cortisone and sex hormones in the body. However, cholesterol can also build up in the blood vessels, making passage of blood difficult. *Unsaturated* fatty acids, which are either monounsaturated or polyunsaturated, are those which are usually liquid at room temperature and are mainly from vegetable sources. These do not raise the blood cholesterol. In fact, the polyunsaturated fats tend to lower the blood cholesterol levels. However they should not be taken in excessive amounts.

What are they used for?
Fats are absolutely necessary for proper brain development and functioning. They are also necessary for the absorption of the fat-soluble vitamins, A, D, E, and K, and for the utilization of calcium and other fat-soluble nutrients. Fats aid in hormone development. They are necessary for the proper functioning and development of the nerves.

How much do we need?
Approximately 25 percent of a child's daily caloric intake should be from fat sources.

What are the signs of deficiency?
Since the oil-soluble vitamins (A, D, E, and K) are stored in body fat, deficiencies in dietary fat can lead to deficiencies in those vitamins.

VITAMIN A

What is it?

Vitamin A is an oil-soluble vitamin that is stored in body fat. It is measured in "international units" (I.U.). In order for it to be properly absorbed, there must be a sufficient supply of fats and minerals in your child's diet. A fat-free diet, or the exclusive use of skim milk, can lead to an insufficient absorption of Vitamin A. Long-term use of mineral oil interferes with absorption of the vitamin. There are two forms of vitamin A. One form is retinol, which is found in animal foods. The second is carotene, which is found basically in plants.

What is it used for?

Vitamin A is necessary for maintaining normal epithelial tissue throughout the body. This tissue includes the cornea and conjunctiva of the eyes. Vitamin A helps tone the mucous membranes of the body. The body's ability to resist infection is dependent upon adequate intake of it. It is a necessary nutrient enabling the eye to adapt efficiently to changes in light intensity. Excessive amounts of vitamin A can be harmful. It can compete with vitamin E and has been implicated in some eye disorders such as macula degeneration.

How do we obtain it?

Retinol is obtained from liver, eggs, cod liver oil, whole milk (but not skim milk), and cheese. Carotene can be obtained from spinach, turnips, beets, lettuce, parsley, carrots, sweet potatoes, and melons.

How much do we need?

Optimal daily amounts by age are considered to be:

From birth to six months:	1,500 I.U.
From six months to one year:	2,000 I.U.
From one year to four years:	5,000 I.U.
From four years to ten years:	15,000 I.U.

What are the signs of deficiency?
- Difficulty in adjusting to different light intensities, especially darkness
- Dry, lusterless look to the conjunctiva and cornea
- Unhealthy hair, skin, teeth, and gums
- Increased respiratory infections
- Dry skin and dandruff (which may also be the symptoms of excessive vitamin A)
- Burning, itching, and inflamed eyes
- Possibilities of styes blepharitis (inflammation of the eyelids), and overactivity of the Meibomian glands (sebaceous glands in the eyelids)

Inadequate intakes of zinc can interfere with the action of vitamin A. Because of the inhibitory action of iron on the oil-soluble vitamins, it is best to take them at opposite ends of the day or at least four hours apart. Do not give vitamin A for at least two hours before strenuous physical activity. Since excess vitamin A is not excreted but is stored in body fat, there is a possibility of overdose. Research indicates, however, that massive quantities of vitamin A supplements would have to be taken over a period of time before symptoms of overdose appeared. Toxic signs may occur with chronic intake of 100,000 I.U. per day in an adult and 20,000 I.U. per day in an infant or child.

THIAMINE (VITAMIN B₁)

What is it?
Thiamine is a water-soluble vitamin that is readily passed through the body. Excess amounts are not stored but are excreted. It is measured in milligrams. Magnesium is necessary for its metabolism. Thiamine is easily lost in cooking through heat, or when caffeine is consumed. It is also lost when taking aspirin or antacids containing aluminum and magnesium hydroxides. The use of cough syrups with alcohol content and the ingestion of excessive amounts of sugar can deplete vitamin B_1.

What is it used for?
Thiamine is a co-enzyme that helps in the metabolism of carbohydrates. It helps the functioning of muscles and the nervous system.

How do we obtain it?
Sources of thiamine include beef, heart, liver, avocados, legumes, nuts, whole grains, and oatmeal.

How much do we need?
Adequate daily amounts by age are considered to be:

From birth to six months:	0.5 mg
From six months to one year:	0.7 mg
From one year to four years:	0.7 mg
From four years to ten years:	2.0 mg

What are the signs of deficiency?
- Dry, burning sensation in the eye and conjunctiva
- Unclear vision
- Inflammation of internal eye tissues
- Inflammation of ocular nerves
- Apathy
- Nystagmus (involuntary oscillation of the eyeball), double vision, and weakening of ocular muscles

RIBOFLAVIN (VITAMIN B$_2$)

What is it?
Riboflavin is a water-soluble vitamin that readily passes through the body. Excessive amounts are not stored but are excreted. It is measured in milligrams. Riboflavin is destroyed by ultraviolet light and the use of tetracyclines.

What is it used for?
Riboflavin is used in tissue oxidation and in respiration. It helps in the metabolism of proteins, carbohydrates, and fats. It promotes the healthy growth of hair, skin, and nails. It is needed by the adrenal glands to produce cortisol (hydrocortisone). It is necessary during periods of stress.

How do we obtain it?
Sources for obtaining riboflavin include meat, liver, heart, kidney, fish, oysters, eggs, milk, cheese, yogurt, peas, asparagus, and almonds.

How much do we need?
Adequate daily amounts by age are considered to be:

From birth to six months:	0.6 mg
From six months to one year:	0.8 mg
From one year to four years:	0.8 mg
From four years to ten years:	2.0 mg

What are the signs of deficiency?
- An infiltration of blood vessels into the cornea
- Cloudiness of ocular tissues
- Cataracts
- Burning and itching of eyes
- Sensitivity to light and increased tearing
- Reduced visual acuity
- Congestion of the sclera (the fibrous outer layer of the eyeball)
- Increased pigmentation of the iris
- Gritty sensation in the eyelids
- Cracks at the corner of the mouth
- A sore tongue
- Scaly skin around the nose and mouth

NIACIN (VITAMIN B₃)

What is it?

Niacin is a water-soluble vitamin that readily passes through the body. Excess amounts are not stored but are excreted. It is measured in milligrams. Niacin is essential for the synthesis of insulin, cortisone, and sex hormones. It is destroyed by water and the use of tetracyclines. The use of cough syrup containing alcohol tends to deplete the niacin in a child's body. Caution should be exercised in the amounts of niacin taken when children are diabetic or have glaucoma, ulcers, or liver problems.

What is it used for?

Niacin is a co-enzyme in glycolysis (the conversion of carbohydrates into energy) and in tissue respiration. It dilates the blood vessels and increases the flow of blood to the peripheral capillary system. In large doses, it lowers levels of plasma cholesterol, triglycerides, and free fatty acids.

How do we obtain it?

Food sources for obtaining niacin include seafood, fish, fowl, dairy products, legumes, whole wheat, mushrooms, figs, dates, and brewer's yeast.

How much do we need?

Adequate daily amounts by age are considered to be:

From birth to six months:	8 mg
From six months to one year:	9 mg
From one year to four years:	10 mg
From four years to ten years:	20 mg

What are the signs of deficiency?

- Dermatitis
- Diarrhea
- Confused thinking
- Irritability
- Chronic headaches
- Disorientation

PANTOTHENIC ACID

What is it?
Pantothenic acid is a water-soluble vitamin that readily passes through the body. Excess amounts are not stored but are excreted. It is measured in milligrams. It is essential for maintaining normal skin, normal growth, and normal development of the nervous system. Pantothenic acid is destroyed by heat, canning, caffeine, and sulfur drugs.

What is it used for?
Pantothenic acid is needed for the proper working of adrenal hormones and for the production of antibodies. It helps to ease soreness and achiness of muscles. It helps reduce the toxic effects of antibiotics. It promotes healing and helps the body withstand stress.

How do we obtain it?
Pantothenic acid is obtained from food sources such as beef, chicken, egg yolk, liver, kidney, legumes, broccoli, cauliflower, mushrooms, nuts, and bran.

How much do we need?
Adequate daily amounts by age are considered to be:

From birth to six months:	5 mg
From six months to one year:	5 mg
From one year to four years:	10 mg
From four years to ten years:	10 mg

What are the symptoms of deficiency?
- Dermatitis
- Diarrhea
- Nausea
- Abdominal pain and cramps
- Fatigue
- Low blood sugar
- Allergic reactions

PYRIDOXINE (VITAMIN B$_6$)

What is it?
Pyridoxine is a water-soluble vitamin that is readily absorbed in the body. The excess is excreted within eight hours after ingestion. It is measured in milligrams. Pyridoxine is essential for the production of antibodies and the development of red blood cells. It is destroyed by long-term storage, canning, and roasting and stewing of meats. It is also destroyed by alcohol, such as is found in some children's cough syrup.

What is it used for?
Pyridoxine is used in the metabolism of proteins and essential fatty acids. It is involved in the production of antibodies and is essential for the synthesis and proper use of DNA and RNA. Pyridoxine is a natural diuretic and regulates the balance between sodium and potassium in the body. It is required for the absorption of vitamin B$_{12}$.

How do we obtain it?
Sources of pyridoxine include food sources such as rare meat, liver, fish, shellfish, and raw leafy vegetables, cabbage, cantaloupe, raw stringbeans, raw fresh sweet peas, corn, and whole grains.

How much do we need?
Adequate daily amounts by age are considered to be:

From birth to six months:	0.7 mg
From six months to one year:	0.7 mg
From one year to four years:	0.7 mg
From four years to ten years:	2.0 mg

What are the signs of deficiency?

- Flaky dermatitis about the eyes and eyebrows
- Conjunctivitis
- Cheilosis (fissures in the lips) and angular stomatitis (cracks in the skin at the corners of the mouth)
- Hyperirritability
- Anemia
- Loss of muscular control
- Slow learning

COBALAMIN (VITAMIN B$_{12}$)

What is it?
Cobalamin is a water-soluble vitamin. It is not well assimilated through the stomach and needs to be combined with calcium for absorption. It is essential for the normal development of red blood cells. It is measured in micrograms. Cobalamin is destroyed by acids and alkalis, water, ultraviolet light, and alcohol such as is found in some children's cough syrups, and by taking phenobarbital and large doses of vitamin C.

What is it used for?
Vitamin B$_{12}$ helps to maintain concentration and memory, as well as a healthy appetite. It helps in the metabolism of proteins, carbohydrates, and fats, and in the maintenance of the nervous system. It helps in the proper functioning of the thyroid.

How do we obtain it?
Sources of vitamin B$_{12}$ include liver, beef, kidney, shellfish, eggs, cheese, milk, brewer's yeast, kelp, and bee pollen.

How much do we need?
Adequate daily amounts by age are considered to be:

From birth to six months:	3 mcg
From six months to one year:	3 mcg
From one year to four years:	3 mcg
From four years to ten years:	5 mcg

What are the signs of deficiency?
- General weakness
- Nervousness
- Poorly functioning thyroid
- Difficulty in concentration
- Numbness and stiffness
- Focusing difficulty
- Scotoma (blocking of central vision)
- Poor reflexes

VITAMIN C

What is it?
Vitamin C is a water-soluble vitamin that is readily absorbed by the body. Excess amounts are excreted in approximately two to three hours. It is measured in milligrams. Vitamin C is essential for the healthy condition of collagen, the "cement" between cells. The vitamin is destroyed by carbon monoxide, water, cooking, heat, ultraviolet light, the use of tetracyclines, and the long-term use of mineral oils. Aspirin triples the rate of excretion of vitamin C.

What is it used for?
Vitamin C is used in oxidation and in cellular respiration. It is used to maintain normal capillary permeability. It protects the body from physical and mental stress and from the toxic effects of cadmium and other chemicals and drugs. It is involved in carbohydrate metabolism and helps the adrenal glands to function. It is important for the absorption of iron.

How do we obtain it?
Sources of vitamin C include citrus fruits, strawberries, melons, tomatoes, green and leafy vegetables, cabbage, peppers, and sweet vegetables and fruit.

How much do we need?
Adequate daily amounts by age are considered to be:

From birth to six months:	40 mg
From six months to one year:	40 mg
From one year to four years:	50 mg
From four years to ten years:	60 mg

What are the signs of deficiency?
- General weakness
- Swollen joints
- Hemorrhages
- Impaired collagen formation
- Sudden onset of exophthalmos (bulging of eyes)
- Capillary weakness

VITAMIN D (ERGOSTEROL AND CALCIFEROL)

What is it?
Vitamin D is a fat-soluble vitamin that is stored in the body. It is acquired through the action of ultraviolet light on the oils in the skin, as well as through diet. It is measured in international units. Vitamin D is destroyed by mineral oil and medications such as phenobarbital. Vitamin D works best when it is taken with vitamin A, vitamin C, choline, calcium, and phosphorus.

What is it used for?
Vitamin D helps maintain a balance in the body between calcium and phosphorus. It is essential for the proper functioning of the thyroid gland. Along with calcium, it has been suggested for the treatment of several eye ailments, including keratoconus (protrusion of the cornea) and myopia.

How do we obtain it?
Vitamin D is supplied by sunlight (ultraviolet light) on the skin, fish liver oil, egg yolks, fortified milk, butter, sunflower sprouts, sardines, herrings, and salmon.

How much do we need?
The adequate daily amount is the same for all ages: 400 I.U. Vitamin D can be toxic if taken in excessive doses, especially over 30,000 I.U. *Note*: Children with heart disease should be cautious about taking excessive amounts of vitamin D.

What are the signs of deficiency?
- Retardation of growth
- Lack of vigor
- Muscular weakness
- Deficient assimilation of minerals
- Rickets (abnormal development of bones)

VITAMIN E (TOCOPHEROLS)

What is it?

Vitamin E is a group of fat-soluble substances known as to-copherols. These heavy oils include alpha, beta, gamma, delta, epsilon, zeta, eta, and theta tocopherols. Vitamin E can be stored in the body but the more active forms are quickly depleted. Much of it is excreted in feces. It is measured in international units. Tocopherols are destroyed by heat and freezing, oxygen, iron, chlorine, and mineral oils. *Note*: Children with overactive thyroid, diabetes, high blood pressure, or rheumatic heart condition should be cautious in the amount of vitamin E supplementation.

What is it used for?

Vitamin E is an antioxidant, inhibiting the combination of other substances with oxygen and therefore acting as a preservative. It is needed for healthy red blood cells. It reduces toxicity from excessive vitamin A. Along with selenium, it has been used for the treatment of some cataracts. It may prevent liquid hydroper-oxide formation in the lens of the eye. It is important in main-taining cell membrane permeability in the eye. This is why some practitioners consider it in the treatment of certain retinal con-ditions. It improves circulation of the tiniest capillaries. It im-proves glycogen storage in the muscles. Vitamin E is necessary for the synthesis of DNA and RNA.

How do we obtain it?

Sources of vitamin E include wheat germ oil, soybean oil, whole wheat, nuts, green leafy vegetables, and eggs.

How much do we need?

Adequate daily amounts by age are considered to be:

From birth to six months:	10 I.U.
From six months to one year:	10 I.U.
From one year to four years:	10 I.U.
From four years to ten years:	30 I.U.

What are the signs of deficiency?
- Muscular disorders
- Fragile red blood cells
- Possibly anemia in premature or low-birth-weight infants
- Abnormal calcium deposits in soft tissues
- Increase of bilirubin (a pigment occurring in bile) in the blood
- Anemia in premature infants

CALCIUM

What is it?
Calcium is an inorganic element that remains as ash after food has been burned. It is a mineral essential for all vital functions of the body. Excess amounts are excreted in feces. Absorption may be substantially reduced by large quantities of fat and by oxalic acid, which is found in chocolate, and phytic acid as in bran. Calcium is measured in milligrams.

What is it used for?
Calcium is used for all muscle activity and for the building of normal bones and teeth. It helps the body use iron. It helps in the transmission of neural impulses. A deficiency of calcium is considered to be one of the reasons for the change in ocular tissues during the development of myopia and keratoconus (protrusion of the cornea).

How do we obtain it?
Sources of calcium include milk, cheese, raw vegetables, oats, almonds, salmon, and sardines.

How much do we need?
Desirable daily amounts by age are considered to be:

From birth to six months:	600 mg
From six months to one year:	600 mg
From one year to four years:	800 mg
From four years to ten years:	1000 mg

What are the signs of deficiency?
- Muscular pains
- Increases in myopia

CHROMIUM

What is it?
Chromium is a mineral needed in trace amounts in the body. It is measured in micrograms. It is part of many enzymes and hormones. White sugar in the diet tends to deplete the body's supply.

What is it used for?
Chromium acts as a cofactor with insulin, which is needed to remove glucose from the blood for use in the cells. It is essential for the proper use of sugar and fat in the body. It helps supply protein where it is needed.

How do we obtain it?
Sources of chromium include whole grains, meat, corn oil, brewer's yeast, and all sweet and starchy fruits and vegetables (mushrooms and shellfish, while rich in chromium, are also rich in its principal antagonist, vanadium).

How much do we need?
Minimal daily amounts are considered to be up to 10 micrograms for children up to one year and up to 60 micrograms for children between one year and four years. For children four to ten, 80 mcg is usually recommended.

What are the signs of deficiency?
New research indicates that a lack of chromium is one of the factors in the development of visual focusing problems and of myopia.

ZINC

What is it?
Zinc is a mineral responsible for the proper maintenance of enzymes. It is depleted by the use of cough syrups containing alcohol and of tetracyclines. It is measured in milligrams.

What is it used for?
Zinc helps enzymes during digestion and metabolism of carbohydrates. It affects tissue respiration and is found in all of the eye's tissues, muscles, and nerves, including the retina, choroid, ciliary body, iris, optic nerves, sclera, cornea, and lens. It is needed for the proper metabolism of vitamin A.

How do we obtain it?
Sources of zinc include milk, eggs, onions, green leafy vegetables, and pumpkin seeds. Phytates in wheat germ reduce the availability of zinc unless the wheat germ is presoaked 30 minutes or more before ingesting.

How much do we need?
Desirable daily amounts by age are considered to be:

From birth to six months:	5 mg
From six months to one year:	5 mg
From one year to four years:	10 mg
From four years to ten years:	15 mg

What are the signs of deficiency?
A deficiency of zinc depresses protein synthesis, which will result in decreased collagen in muscles and connective tissue. Authorities feel that zinc metabolism is related to learning problems and that learning-disabled children can be distinguished by their increased levels of lead and cadmium, and decreased levels of zinc. Deficiency signs include:
• White spots on nails
• Poor attention
• Fatigue
• Loss of interest in learning

IRON

What is it?
Iron is a mineral that is essential to the formation of hemoglobin (red blood corpuscles) and myoglobin (red pigment in muscles). It is necessary for the transport of oxygen from the lungs to the tissues. Lack of iron is one of the most common nutrient deficiencies in the school-age child. Excessive phosphorus reduces its availability. It is measured in milligrams.

What is it used for?
Iron is used in the metabolism of the B vitamins. It builds up the quality of blood. The absorption of iron is helped by vitamin C. Iron is depleted by the use of cough syrup containing alcohol, by antacids, and by tetracyclines.

How do we obtain it?
Sources of iron include apricots, bananas, prunes, raisins, brewer's yeast, liver, raw clams, and red meats.

How much do we need?
The recommended daily amount for all children appears to be 18 milligrams.

What are the signs of deficiency?
• Rundown feeling
• Muscular weakness
• Lack of attentiveness
• Lowered school performance

No additive shall be deemed to be safe if it is found to induce cancer when ingested by man or animal, or if it is found, after tests which are appropriate for the evaluation of food additives, to induce cancer in man or animals.

—Amendment to Food,
Drug & Cosmetic Act, 1958

Food Additives to Avoid

ANTIOXIDANTS

Antioxidants are used to prevent foods from getting rancid and fruits from browning. They control the growth of mold, bacteria, and yeast. They are generally in packaged products that may have lost their nutrients by the time of purchase. They're found in vegetable shortenings, puddings, pie filling mixes, canned and frozen food, bread, cookies, and cheese. Examples: BHT, BHA, propyl gallate.

EMULSIFIERS

Emulsifiers allow foods to maintain their consistency and texture by dispensing tiny globules of one liquid into another. They are found in salad dressing, margarine, cake, pies, mixes, chocolate, and bread. Examples: BVO (brominated vegetable oil), propylene glycol monostearate.

STABILIZERS AND THICKENERS

Stabilizers and thickeners are used to maintain a smooth and uniform texture. They are found in ice cream, cream cheese, frozen desserts, baked goods, jams, and jellies.

COLORINGS

Colorings are used to enhance the appearance of foods, soft drinks, soft-drink mixes, candies, jam, jellies, and pie fillings.

Be especially careful of the following items in your children's food: artificial coloring Orange B, used in hot dogs; Red No. 40, used in soda, candy, and desserts: Red No. 3, used in cherries (in fruit cocktail) and candy; BHT and BHA, antioxidants used in cereals and potato chips; saccharin, a noncaloric sweetener used in soda, diet foods, and toothpaste; sodium nitrites or nitrates, used in bacon, ham, and luncheon meats; monosodium glutamate (MSG) used in soups, sauces, and Chinese foods; propyl gallate, an antioxidant used in soups; and sodium bisulfite, a preservative used in wine, grape juice, and dried fruits.

Since not enough is known about the long-term effects of these additives, or of their effects upon each other, the safest route is avoidance when possible. Some of them have been shown to cause cancer in laboratory animals.

PART THREE

VISION IN TROUBLE

10
What Makes a Child Vulnerable?

Growth is a process of organization. It is a
unitary and an integrative process. If it were
not unitary, the organism would lack
wholeness; if it were not integrative, the
organism would lack individuality.

—Dr. Arnold Gesell

As I came into the examination room, I saw the three of them: Grandma with a defiantly guilty look on her face, Father with a stern visage that only partially masked his controlled anger, and Mother with that perplexed anxiety that only mothers can exhibit. In the examination chair sat Alex, defeat weighing on his little shoulders and a face that said, "What did I do to deserve this?"

Before I could complete my examination, I was bombarded by questions as well as answers concerning how little Alex could have gotten into this mess. Grandmother wanted to know if she could have passed on the gene that was responsible for Alex's visual problem. She also wanted to be sure that I knew that the only one in her family who had had a visual problem was her second cousin, Samantha. But she didn't think that second cousins counted. Father, on the other hand, felt that it was Alex's fault. He didn't eat properly, he didn't work hard enough at school, and he watched too much TV with his face pressed up against the screen. Mother said she felt that she was probably at fault. She was nervous during her pregnancy and she smoked heavily. One of her neighbors had told her that a friend of hers had heard that a woman down the hall, who had smoked during her pregnancy, gave birth to children who have learning problems.

Everyone thinks he has the explanation for problems such as Alex's. Unfortunately, the truth is that we really do not know the cause of some visual difficulties such as inaccurate tracking, sluggish focusing, incomplete binocularity, or the visual confusions that affect academic work. We do know what happens when a mother contracts German measles in the first or second trimester of pregnancy. We also know what happens when the hospital gives a premature child too much oxygen. We're beginning to know the side effects of medications that are prescribed to help women through difficult pregnancies. Unfortunately, there are times when we realize the side effects far too late to do anything about them. We also know the effects of physical trauma, such as when a baby accidentally rolls off the dressing room table and hits his head. In all of these instances, the cause of the child's problem is quite clear. For the child with visual coordination problems and visual perception problems, we are just guessing. We're using statistics to try to reveal the probable cause.

Instead of looking for a single cause for these vision problems, it would be more profitable to look at the overall scheme of development, including genetic and environmental influences, to understand how the vulnerable child got that way. The long period of pregnancy and infancy serves to ensure that the child is supplied with the necessary conditions to survive and to perpetuate the race. Although each individual is endowed with a degree of modifiability, the world we were fitted for is not the world we live in. We only have to look at the changes that have occurred in modern times in our nutrition, in our ways of living and working, in our daily activities, in the effects of smoking and drinking on our health and our growth, and in our use—our overuse—of medications and drugs. We should also look at the changes in the type of stress that we're involved in and how we deal with that stress if we are to begin to see that we live in a far different world than the one our ancestors lived in. However, we come into this world equipped as they were.

With the increasing sophistication of medical science and the continued health education of the general population, many illnesses have just about disappeared. The infant mortality rate, which stood at 140 in every 1,000 births in the early 1900s, was 11.2 for every 1000 live births in 1982. Many children survive early childhood illnesses with apparently only minor side effects. Those same illnesses in earlier times would have led to serious complications and perhaps death.

Today, with the help of modern medical science, children with genetic abnormalities and birth complications are aided in their struggle to survive. Children who in another day would not have survived grow up today to be functioning adults. But they also represent a large part of the group of vulnerable people we see with vision problems, learning problems, and difficulty coping.

An individual's hereditary endowment plays a very important role in guiding the course of his or her growth and development. Now that scientists have developed the means of dissecting the human genetic code, we are beginning to obtain a much clearer picture of the role that genetics plays in illnesses. Each human cell has approximately 100,000 genes, which are, in fact, minute chemical factories, arranged in a linear sequence in each chromosome. Each gene is responsible for a specific trait and is located in a specific place in the chromosome. Within each chromosome there is a long, chainlike molecule known as DNA (deoxyribonucleic acid). DNA holds in place pairs of chemicals called nucleotide bases. There are four different chemical units—adenine, thymine, cytosine, and guanine—which are arranged in a specific sequence. These form the genetic code that controls growth and development by directing the chemical processes that ultimately result in different body structures.

The genetic code, then, is a specific sequence of the four different chemicals. Let's call them A, T, C, and G. Genetic defects occur with a "misspelling" of the code that has been inherited or caused by some chemical change. By unlocking the genetic code, scientists are beginning to understand the basis of inherited diseases, such as sickle-cell anemia. They are also becoming aware that some adult diseases may be the result of a predisposition that can be traced to chromosome irregularities. These diseases, then, are a mixture of genetic predispositions and environmental stresses. Although genetic counseling is important for some families—especially when there is a strong familial possibility—it should be borne in mind that *statistical probabilities are not definite eventualities.* Genes indicate the *potentiality* for a trait. A very important second part of that equation, though, is the environment in which the individual grows up. And that includes the environment of the developing embryo. What happens in the womb can aid or hinder the inherited tendencies of the developing person.

The embryo develops very quickly after the egg is fertilized. In the first trimester, the fetus's organs are being formed, even though at the end of three months it only weighs one ounce and is only about three inches long. The visual system begins to develop at three weeks. By four weeks, the lens of the eye starts to develop. By six weeks, the retina is beginning to develop. At seven weeks, traces of nerve fibers reach the eye and the eyelids are beginning to form. At ten weeks, the iris and the focusing mechanism begin to develop. Tear glands also begin their development at this time. By the sixteenth week, the eyes can look very much as we would expect them to look.

During the second trimester, the embryo reaches a length of about twelve inches and weighs about one and one-half pounds. The baby is almost completely formed. He has ears, eyelids, lashes, brows, teeth, and toenails. He now begins to move. He opens and closes his eyes. The third trimester provides the finishing touches. It is during this period that the retinal layers are completed and become light-perceptive.

The uterus provides an ideal protective environment for the fetus to grow, but it must be remembered that it is an especially critical time for the developing individual. He is vulnerable to all sorts of stresses. These include alcohol and nicotine that the mother may take into her system. They include the reduction of available proteins, vitamins, and minerals that she may not be supplying. Also included are the effects of any medication she is on and the results of hormones she releases because she is under stress. If you are to help prevent a developmental problem, it is necessary that your pregnancy be a happy one, in which you keep a keen eye on the things your child needs in order to be born healthy. Each year, 250,000 babies are born with developmental defects. It has been stated that 75 percent of these developmental problems can be attributed to some environmental agent or factor. The accompanying table lists the most common environmental causes.

Environmental Causes of Birth Defects

1. Radiation (therapeutic): less than 1 percent of birth defects
2. Infections: approximately 2 to 3 percent of birth defects
   a. Rubella
   b. Cytomegalovirus
   c. Herpes
   d. Toxoplasmosis
   e. Syphilis
3. Metabolic Causes
   a. Diabetes
   b. Phenylketonuria
4. Drugs: approximately 2 to 3 percent of birth defects
   a. Androgenic hormone
   b. Folic acid antagonists
   c. Thalidomide
   d. Organic mercury
   e. Hypoglycemics
   f. Anticonvulsants

THE HAZARDS OF DRUGS

We are today, as never before, a drug society. It is estimated that 90 percent of all pregnant women take one or more drugs, ranging from aspirin to barbiturates. Their dangerous side effects are just beginning to be revealed.

The world slowly awoke to the dangers of drugs taken by pregnant women during the early 1960s when there was a catastrophic outbreak of phocomelia (seal limbs). Children were born without arms and legs or with flipperlike stumps. Everyone breathed a sigh of relief when the sedative thalidomide was found to be the cause. Yet today, despite what we learned from the thalidomide disaster, pregnant women take an average of four drugs during their pregnancies. Some of these drugs have aroused suspicion from medical research. They include popular tranquilizers such as chlorpromazine (Thorazine) and meprobamate (Miltown, Equanil) as well as antibiotics and sulfur drugs. Even salicylates (aspirin) are not free from suspicion. All of these drugs pass through the placenta to the fetus. In laboratory animals they have been shown to induce malformations of various organs, including the eyes.

Common Drugs Suspected of Causing Developmental Defects

1. Tranquilizers
   a. Chlorpromazine
   b. Meprobamate
   c. Reserpine
2. Antibiotics and Sulfur Drugs
   a. Penicillin
   b. Streptomycin
   c. Actinomycin D
   d. Terramycin
   e. Sulfanilamide
   f. Sulfadiazine
3. Others
   a. Aminopterin
   b. Thiadiazole
   c. Meclizine
   d. Quinine
   e. Insulin
   f. Salicylates (aspirin)
   g. Steroid hormones (androgen and estrogen)

Unfortunately, many women do not realize they are pregnant during the early, critical phases of development, which would include the first two months. Therefore, women in the childbearing years should be cautious about taking drugs if there is a chance of becoming pregnant. Sometimes the effects of drugs that the pregnant woman takes are not seen immediately. They may show up later as hyperactivity, allergies, visual difficulties, or more serious conditions. Women under treatment for cramps, bleeding, or possible miscarriage were once give DES (diethylstilbestrol)—a drug whose disastrous effects did not show up until some fifteen years later, when daughters of those women developed a rare form of vaginal cancer.

Sometimes, a delayed effect on the child's development can come from nondrug causes many, many years later. There are studies that indicate that a mother who has grown up in poverty, or with severe malnutrition as a child, can pass on an unsupportive uterine environment to her daughter, that finally shows up as a problem in her grandchild.

Drugs that appear to have no effect on adults may have disastrous effects on a three- to twelve-inch, one-ounce to one-pound fetus. Drugs are generally given according to body weight, but what is a minimum dose for you can be a mammoth one for your baby. This is true for the whole range of anesthetics, sedatives, and tranquilizers given for obstetrical reasons. There have been reports that children born with the aid of obstetrical medication demonstrate a difficulty in controlling their crying even when they are comforted. They also tend to show interference in developing cognitive skills. Anesthesia tends to lessen and weaken the frequency of labor contractions. This may make it more difficult for the child to get through the birth canal. Perhaps Lamaze had the right idea: What mothers need is the loving support of their husbands during labor and delivery. They need training in relaxation, breathing exercises, and a good understanding of what to expect.

SMOKING

It used to be rare to see a woman smoking. Today it is not uncommon to walk into a restaurant and find more women smoking than men. Some researchers are beginning to think that the main reason for the different life expectancies between men and women is the number of smokers in each group. Perhaps it is coincidental, but as more women take up smoking, the difference between the life expectancies of the sexes has decreased.

Smoking appears to be related both to the number of premature births and to the number of low birth weights recorded every year. Each has been found in a high percentage of children with visual-perceptual problems and learning difficulties. Nicotine is a vasoconstrictor; in other words, it narrows the blood vessels and thus reduces blood flow. Approximately fifteen minutes must pass after smoking for the effects to wear off. During smoking, carbon monoxide enters the bloodstream and reduces the level of oxygen available to the fetus. There are reports that women who smoke an average of ten cigarettes a day have appreciably smaller babies than nonsmokers. Also, some recent evidence, involving sudden infant death syndrome, implicates smoking during pregnancy.

One beautiful day, as I was driving along the East River Drive in New York City admiring all the beautiful people jogging between the river and the traffic, I was startled to hear a report on the radio. They had just measured the amount of carbon monoxide ingested by those very same joggers. They found that people who jogged alongside heavy traffic ingested significantly higher amounts of carbon monoxide than people who jogged far away from traffic. It occured to me that not only should joggers try to find places where there is clear air, but that pregnant women should also avoid frequenting places that are saturated with carbon monoxide.

ALCOHOL

Not only have women taken up smoking, but they have also increased their rate of alcohol consumption. Although a drink may relax you, it can also alter enzyme activities and lead to reduced birth size and weight. The use of alcohol by pregnant woman is reportedly related to premature births. Women who are heavy drinkers have been shown to have a greater chance of having children with birth defects. But how much is too much? It appears that four or more ounces a day is too much in this respect. There is evidence that just one evening of heavy drinking during the first trimester of pregnancy can result in a child with a developmental defect. As a society, we're just beginning to fully realize these facts. As I write this, New York City has passed an ordinance that in every place where drink is served, a sign should be put up indicating the dangers of drinking, especially for pregnant women.

INFECTIONS

Sometimes birth defects occur because the mother was the unfortunate recipient of an infection or virus. Conditions such as mumps, hepatitis, vaccinia, herpes simplex, measles, or cytomegalovirus contracted during the first six months can have serious consequences. We do not know the results of infections contracted within the last trimester.

STRESS

Pregnancy is usually a happy time. Sometimes, however, a pregnant mother experiences prolonged periods of emotional stress. Chronically high levels of emotional stress appear to contribute to an increase in the incidence of prematurity and delivery problems, as well as lead to behavioral disturbances in infancy and early childhood. Prolonged stress stimulates the sympathetic nervous system, which arouses the adrenal, pituitary, and thyroid glands. They release adrenaline, noradrenaline, and cortisone. This results in a change in blood pressure and in the amount of fat that is released into the bloodstream. There are also changes in the level of sugar, potassium, and sodium. The immune system can become suppressed, so that the mother is susceptible to all kinds of infections, affecting the functioning in the fetus. It has been noted that infectious diseases and accidents occur with much greater frequency during and after periods of stress.

Pregnancy should be a time for nonsense, for poetry, and happy thoughts. One way to deal with negative feelings is to write them down. Share them with your partner and try to work them out. Another way to deal with negative feelings is to practice visualizing happy events. For this, I have included, at the end of the chapter, a suggested receptive visualization routine.

COMPLICATIONS IN DELIVERY

A baby may have had a good environment during pregnancy, but then run into difficulty during or shortly after delivery. The most usual causes are complications of the baby's position during delivery, which delayed birth and resulted in a lack of needed oxygen. We see this in breech births and sometimes instrument deliveries. Occasionally, there is a compression of the umbilical cord or of the child's head coming through the birth canal. During multiple births, children who are not the first born compete for the available nutrition and oxygen. The further away they are from first born, the more difficulty they tend to have. Unusual as it may sound, children who are delivered by cesarean section, when labor is less than two hours, have been found also to have difficulty. The reason may be that they were thrust out into an oxygen environment too early for them to adapt appropriately.

The following is a list of risk conditions at birth.

- Premature birth (less than 38 weeks)
- Low birth weight (delivery under 5½ pounds)
- Breech birth
- Delayed delivery
- A labor of less than two hours
- Multiple births
- Complications with the umbilical cord
- An unusual position during birth
- A body length of less than 18½ inches
- A head circumference of less than 13 inches
- A low Apgar rating (an estimate of the infant's condition one to five minutes after birth)

THE APGAR SCORE

Observations and scoring of five vital signs are obtained one and five minutes after birth. In cesarean births, it may be repeated every five minutes for fifteen minutes.

The optimal score is 10. The lower the score, the greater the possibility of future difficulties. A score of 4 or less warrants immediate attention.

SIGN	SCORE 0	SCORE 1	SCORE 2
Heart Rate	Absent	Below 100	Over 100
Respiration	Absent	Irregular	Good Crying
Reflex Response	No Response	Grimace	Good Response
Color	Blue/Pale	Pink Body/ Blue Extremities	Completely Pink
Muscle Tone	Flaccid	Weak	Strong

While all these possibilities for difficulties sound as if pregnancy were a minefield for the mother to traverse, rest assured that the greatest number of pregnancies are uneventful. Knowing what could happen should not lead you to despair. It should only serve to remind you of the things to avoid. If something should occur, it does not by itself guarantee that your child will experience some visual difficulty or other problem. It only means that you will have to watch him carefully and make sure that you supply an enriched environment in order to optimize his growth.

VISUALIZATION PROCEDURE

Find a quiet place where you will be undisturbed for at least ten minutes. Look at something that you feel is beautiful, or that makes you feel good. If you do not have anything to look at, just gently close your eyes.

Breathe in and out so that your abdomen rises and falls. Let your breathing become slow and even. Shortly you will feel peaceful.

Now imagine that you are being gently cradled and lifted by a colorful balloon. It gently lifts you and takes you above your home so that you can see people, family, and yourself.

Imagine seeing yourself with your new baby. See yourself enjoying yourself. Listen to your baby gurgling. Watch your baby smile at you. Let yourself smell baby lotion and feel the soft velvety touch of baby skin.

Enjoy the scene. Be part of the scene with all your senses. Let it make you feel alive and fulfilled.

At other times visualize the happiness of your child at different ages. Your baby's first encounter with a bath, another baby, your baby on a swing, on a bicycle, going to school. See yourself and your baby smiling, laughing, and enjoying a good life, a healthy life.

Return to your pictures as often as you like.

11
What Parents Can Do: Preventing and Identifying Problems

There are four keys to helping ensure optimal development for your child. The first is to *learn to be the primary diagnostician*, so to speak. This involves noting your child's development and comparing it to developmental norms. When you do this, you should keep in mind that many children vary from these norms without being in serious trouble. However, if there appears to be a lag in development which persists over a period of time, and the delay appears to be below the norm by approximately 25 percent or greater, then I feel it is time to have your child looked at professionally. As an example: if the average time for your child to walk unsupported is fifteen months, then a 25 percent delay means that the child did not walk until nineteen months. This does not mean that a child who walks at nineteen months will have difficulty. It only means that the child should be looked at carefully to see if his overall gross motor skills are also showing a similar delay. Sometimes these delays are only individual differences in development that shortly reverse themselves without any obvious problems. However, sometimes they are early signs of later visual or perceptual problems. It is best to check them early and provide simple, non-anxiety-provoking games to stimulate development.

The second key is to *provide the best possible environment for growth*. This involves good nutrition, the absence of an allergic atmosphere and allergic food substances, and the availability of loving parents—both father and mother, and if possible, grandparents, too. It means that mother has to be given the opportunity to rest so that she can respond to her child in a natural, fun-loving way, free of the stress and irritability of fatigue. It also means that the child should have plenty of opportunities to explore his senses and what they tell him about his environment. There should be nightlights to look at. There should be an unrestricted space to explore that is safe, and not too much bundling up that restricts free and easy movement. The child should have toys that allow opportunities to experience different textures, sounds, patterns, and movements. These toys should be shatterproof and non-flammable, with no sharp points or spring-loaded parts. Be particularly mindful of any toy that can cause a sharp or blunt trauma to the eye. Your child should have an opportunity to develop skills so that he can take pleasure from his increased mastery of those skills.

Because most children seem to develop naturally, we tend to overlook what goes into developing a seemingly natural skill. Several years ago, a research project explored what would happen if a laboratory animal was allowed to see its environment and be moved around its environment, but was not allowed to move around its environment at its own initiative. In this experiment, one kitten was free to walk around, while a second kitten was carried in a cradle so that it moved at the same speed as the first animal. Both animals viewed the same scenery. The result was that the animal that was not able to move around on its own initiative, making its own judgments of where it was going, how fast, and what happened, became significantly immature in spatial perception compared with the one that had the freedom to explore and control its own movements through space. A second experiment allowed the animal to freely walk around, but did not allow it to see its paws as it walked. This was accomplished by having it wear a very wide collar that blocked its view of its paws. The result was that it did not develop normal eye-paw coordination. Both of these experiments reveal what can happen to children who have their visual motor development interrupted or interfered with because of an illness (during a critical learning period) or because they are continually unsuccessful in visual-motor activities. Children who are expected to perform above their skill levels and who are under pressure to perform, never have the freedom to explore tasks and develop their own unique methods.

Disrupted development can also occur because a child is not allowed to participate in the usual rough and tumble play of childhood for fear of injury. This results in a lack of skill development and antipathy to participation in visual-motor activities. Later we see such children having difficulty in such human tasks as writing, catching a ball, batting, playing tennis, skiing, and so on. They are a reminder that children should be given the opportunity to explore their environment on their own.

The third key that helps ensure optimal development is to *find a developmentally trained optometrist* who can work with infants and communicate with parents. (See chapter 13.) When you find one, work with him or her. Have the optometrist evaluate your child approximately every six months from birth to three years, and then at least once each year after this—that is, unless there is some problem detected by you or by the doctor. The evaluations provide a profile of visual, perceptual, and general development. As the doctor compares one evaluation to the previous, important lags in visual development can be detected early, and they can be corrected by providing simple visual games to encourage normal visual development.

The fourth key is to *watch your child shortly after experiencing a trauma or a childhood disease.* These periods of debilitation can interfere with completing critical phases of visual development. It is not unusual for a strabismus to develop after a bout with measles, or for myopia to develop after a long period of high fever or a particularly stressful event.

The following reflex and developmental sequences should be used to follow the course of your child's development. Make sure you keep accurate records.

Early Infant Reflexes

If any of the following reflexes fail to disappear at the expected age, consult your doctor.

1. Doll's Eye Phenomenon
   Test this reflex by turning the infant's head to the right or left while the rest of his body is stationary. You should observe

that the eyes stay fixed and do not move with the head. *This reflex should disappear by the end of the first month.*

2. McCarthy's Reflex

Test this reflex by tapping the supraorbital area (above the eyebrow). It produces a blinking of the eye on the side that is tapped. *This reflex should disappear between the second and fourth months.*

3. Moro Reflex

Test this reflex by suddenly banging your hand on a nearby table. The baby will open and extend his arms as if embracing something. *This reflex should disappear between the fourth and sixth months.*

4. Tonic Neck Reflex (TNR)

Test this reflex by turning the baby's head to one side as he lies on his back. The result is an extension of the arm and leg on the same side as the chin, and a flexing of the opposite arm and leg. *This reflex should disappear between the sixth and seventh months.*

5. Neck-Righting Reflex

Test this reflex by turning the baby's head to one side as he lies on his back. The shoulders, then the trunk, and finally the pelvis will turn in the same direction as the turned head. *This reflex should disappear between the ninth and twelfth months.*

Developmental Milestones

SIX MONTHS

1. Turns objects to observe them upside-down and sideways while exploring them visually.
2. Transfers objects from one hand to another.
3. Begins to become aware that objects and people are permanent and present even if they are hidden.
4. Begins to imitate facial expressions and actions.
5. Likes to play games such as Peekaboo and Pat-a-Cake.

EIGHT MONTHS

1. Is able to hold head erect briefly while sitting.
2. Begins to show creeping skills, forward and backward.
3. Begins to pull himself up on familiar objects.

4. Talks or babbles to his toys, expressing demands and socializing with them.
5. Is able to sit with support.
6. Reaches for objects, grasps them, and brings them closer for inspection.
7. Recalls a sequence of events.
8. Begins to recognize his own image in a mirror.
9. Explores his environment with his body, with his eyes, hands, and mouth.
10. Can play with toys for a long period of time.
11. Begins to show fear of strangers.
12. Has a strong attachment for his mother and fears separation from her.

TWELVE MONTHS

1. Can twist his body from side to side as he stands.
2. Participates more in his own feeding.
3. Responds to commands like, "Look at this" and "Give it to me."
4. Repeats familiar words.
5. Vocalizes or names an object while pointing to it.
6. Can put a block in a container and place objects in a line.
7. Begins to scribble with a crayon.
8. Can point to his eye, nose, mouth.
9. Begins to show awareness of himself as separate from others.
10. Begins to recognize emotions that others show.

TWO YEARS

1. Can balance on one foot very briefly.
2. Can jump in place with both feet together.
3. Can walk to a ball and kick it.
4. Can turn the pages in a book.
5. Can respond yes or no when asked, "Is your name———?"
6. Can point to the different parts of a doll (hair, mouth, ears, hands).
7. Understands the concepts *little* and *big*.
8. Can use single words or short phrases of up to four words.
9. Names things, people, actions, and situations.

10. Begins to use plural words to indicate more than one.
11. Can identify pictures of familiar things, such as a baby, a car, or a girl.
12. Begins to sense the meaning of cause and effect.
13. Names himself when he sees himself in a picture.
14. Has difficulty sharing because he considers his possessions to be extensions of himself.
15. May hide his toys to avoid sharing them.
16. Begins to learn the possessive pronoun *mine*.
17. Is just beginning to go beyond parallel play.

THREE YEARS

1. Can change direction sharply when he walks.
2. Can walk downstairs with alternate feet.
3. Can hop on one foot.
4. Can catch and throw large balls.
5. Can grasp a small object with his fingers and begins to button and unbutton.
6. Can unscrew small container caps.
7. Understands the concepts *in*, *under*, and *behind*.
8. Names at least two of the colors red, green, blue, and yellow.
9. Can identify all his body parts by pointing.
10. Can give personal information about himself—name, age, and sex.
11. Uses adverbs of location: "I am going *there*."
12. Uses prepositions (*to, in, on*).
13. Can repeat a four-word sentence or three digits.
14. Can follow two commands involving spatial concepts such as *on, under,* or *behind*.
15. Begins to express himself verbally rather than by acting out his feelings.
16. Can match four basic colors and basic geometric forms.
17. Can string beads.
18. Although interested in playing with other children, he also continues to enjoy playing by himself and in parallel situations.
19. Can sleep through the night without bedwetting.
20. Can help set the table before meals and can complete simple household chores.

FOUR YEARS

1. Can walk smoothly and with a steady gait.
2. Can alternate his feet going upstairs, with help.
3. Begins to show some skipping skills.
4. Can throw a ball with greater precision, and can catch a large ball.
5. Can dress and undress himself with large articles of clothing.
6. Can lace his shoes.
7. Can identify the *same* and *different* in objects presented in pictures.
8. Can identify the longer of two lines and has the concept of *two*.
9. Can name the colors red, green, blue, and yellow.
10. Can repeat four digits and can count to five by rote.
11. Understands the concepts *one, two,* and *many*.
12. Can copy a cross and a square.
13. Shares possessions from home.
14. Brushes his teeth and combs his hair with help.

FIVE YEARS

1. Can balance on one foot, hop on one foot, skip, and march rhythmically.
2. Can make a running broad jump.
3. Can walk up and down the stairs using alternate feet.
4. Can use skates, a sled, and a wagon.
5. Can build with blocks.
6. Can follow a lace pattern board.
7. Can copy a square and a triangle.
8. Understands *first, last,* and *middle*.
9. Understands the concept of *three* and *four*.
10. Can describe a picture.
11. Can make comparisons using the concepts *bigger* and *more*.
12. Can count to ten by rote.
13. Can name a nickel, a penny, and a dime.
14. Can use the pronouns *he, she,* and *they*.
15. Knows his name and address.
16. Is just beginning to understand the whole of something he's looking at. Is still limited to seeing primarily the parts.
17. Can differentiate left and right on himself, but not on others.
18. Can draw a person with a head, trunk, arms, legs, and some facial details.

EYE EMERGENCIES

Blow to the Eye

Because these are common and can result in serious consequences, your child's eye should be examined carefully.

Look carefully to determine if there has been any direct wound to the eyeball itself, or it is merely to the brows. Determine:

1. If there is any cut on the white of the eye.
2. If there is any blood visible in the colored part of the eye.
3. If the eye has been struck by a small object, has something gotten past the brow or cheek area?
4. If there is pain or sensitivity to light even without visible injury. Any of the above require immediate medical attention.

If the above signs or symptoms are not present, then probably immediate attention is not necessary. However, any jarring blow to the head can result in retinal tears and internal injuries. This is especially true if your child reports spots, floating objects, and flashes of light anytime after the injury. To be on the safe side, have your eye doctor check the inside of his eye as soon as possible, at one month and six months after the blow.

If there is no other serious injury except the swelling of the surrounding facial tissues, then use ice packs to reduce the swelling.

Foreign Body

Sometimes sand or dirt can become stuck in your child's cornea (transparent window covering the colored part of the eye) or under the upper lid. Try first to determine if the object has penetrated the eye or merely appears stuck to the surface tissues.

To view the underneath of the upper lid:

1. Hold the eyelashes gently.
2. Have the child look down while you place a cotton-tipped applicator horizontally on the upper lid.
3. Lift the lid up as you apply gentle pressure downward with the applicator.
4. The lid will turn over, allowing you to see if there is any speck of dirt underneath.

If your child's discomfort is from some dirt, then gently squeeze lukewarm water from a bulb syringe onto the eye to see if you can wash it off. If the dirt is on the underside of the upper lid, then you can remove it with a gentle swipe of the cotton-tipped applicator.

Red Eye

The white of the eye should be clear, shining, and white. Sometimes air pollutants, lack of sleep, or allergic reactions can cause the eye to appear red. If there is any crust on the lids or a yellow or green discharge, you should see your doctor. If the redness appears to be due to irritants, such as chlorine in pools, smog or allergies, I find that the best treatment is rest and cold compresses.

Styes

A stye is a small infection on the lid margin. It usually looks red and swollen, like a red pimple. The treatment consists of applying warm compresses to the area every fifteen minutes. After a while the stye will open. Wipe away the liquid that oozes out. Apply an antibacterial eye ointment to prevent the infection from spreading. Your local pharmacist can recommend an over-the-counter ointment.

12
Some Common Visual Problems

Subtract the mind ... and the eye is open to
no purpose, which before did not see.

—Meister Eckhart

MYOPIA

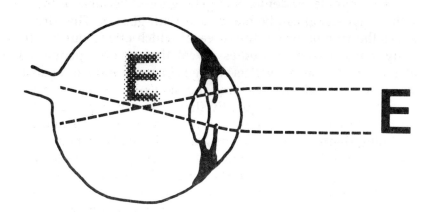

    The visual system is a highly flexible and adaptable system.
Unfortunately, its adaptability can lead to problems. One problem
that occurs is silently reaching epidemic proportions: the problem
of myopia, or nearsightedness.

The myopic person has lost the ability to shift his focus and see distant objects clearly. The focus is stuck at a close distance, called the focal point. Objects seen at the focal point look clear. By increasing his focus, the myopic person can see objects closer to him than his focal point. However, he is unable to relax his focus, so that objects farther than his focal point appear blurred.

Very few children are born with myopia, probably less than 1 percent. As your child progresses in school, especially if he works hard and does well, he is more apt to develop myopia sometime during his school years. By age ten, approximately 6 percent of schoolchildren develop myopia. We are likely to find that 20 percent of eighth-graders are myopic. And by the end of high school, this figure will reach 40 percent. In college, the figures range somewhere between 60 and 80 percent.

These figures can vary depending upon the country you are in and whether you live in an urban or a rural area. They can also vary with occupation and social status. If, for example, you live in Germany or Japan, you will find that the percentages I have cited are too low. As you look at people that live in a rural area, involved primarily in agricultural occupations, you will find fewer people who are myopic. But as soon as you start to examine urban people who do considerable close work, especially performing under tense conditions where they have to be constantly vigilant, then you begin to see a large increase in the number of people who are myopic.

The myopia epidemic is largely ignored because of the ease with which vision can be made clear with glasses. This situation masks the true nature of the disease, which affects our health in many ways. Research studies reveal that myopic people have altered metabolism as well as changes in respiration and galvanic skin response (which measures the skin's resistance to a weak electric current). They frequently show changes in posture, tending to hold tension in the throat, neck, and jaw areas and often exhibiting depression of the chest area. They also report a sense of disconnectedness from their feet. Myopic people are distinctly different on psychological tests, so much so that there is a 70 percent chance of determining who is myopic just by looking at their paper-and-pencil scores. Myopic people are more prone to other eye diseases, such as vitreous changes, retina detachment and possibly even glaucoma and cataracts.

Unfortunately, too many books still refer to myopia as an inherited condition for which there is no known prevention. Imagine being told that 80 percent of the population will develop a heart condition for which nothing can be done except to wait until it occurs and then go to the hospital for a bypass. I know that you wouldn't accept this philosophy. That is the main reason why so many people today are watching what they eat and exercising their bodies. Yet many people accept the view that myopia is unavoidable. They are evidently unaware of the research that has been done in the last fifty years or so, giving us a much clearer picture of the myopic process: what causes it, what influences its course, and how we can prevent and control it. While some cases of myopia can be due to an inherited predisposition, I believe that family life-style, attitudes and expectations, nutrition, and work habits are considerably more important.

Since 1900 there have been numerous psychological studies comparing myopic and nonmyopic people. Most studies reveal a tendency for myopes to be introverted, shy, meticulous people who prefer indoor rather than outdoor activities. Although these studies suggest how the myopic population as a group might behave, the profile is not necessarily true of every individual.

The results of intelligence tests show that myopic people score higher than people who are not myopic. But this is also true for their reading tests and paper-and-pencil tests. It appears therefore that the myopic person may not be more intelligent, but does prefer those very activities that intelligence tests measure, namely, reading, paper-and-pencil activities, and reflection rather than action.

Some researchers believe that myopia develops in order to allow a person to reduce or control what is seen so that he will not be overwhelmed by a flood of visual stimulation. Others believe that the psychological characteristics that myopic people demonstrate are the natural consequence of the development of myopia. It seems to me that certain behavorial styles provide a greater vulnerability to the development of myopia. In a work situation that requires continuous focusing of the eyes at a close distance, people with certain behavorial characteristics will be more apt to stay the course and do well. This type of person will more likely prefer a sedentary situation to a highly active one. He would be better served if he had a high need for achievement.

He also would find the task easier if he were a "sharpener" rather than a "leveler." Sharpeners tend to prefer situations that are precise, concrete, and well defined, instead of vague and generalized. Emotionally he would have tight control over his feelings and especially would passively endure anxiety in order to achieve a goal. The person who had these characteristics would find it easier to stay in a stressful visual situation in order to achieve. A person who didn't have them would find it very difficult to stay involved for long periods of time.

The psychological traits that are usually revealed when testing groups of myopic people may then be the very attitudes, perceptual styles, and emotional characteristics that are necessary to achieve at the very tasks that myopic people love—sitting still, reading, and thinking. That there are people who have these characteristics and are not nearsighted simply means there are other factors which must be present in order for myopia to occur.

What increases your chances of becoming myopic? I have mentioned before that I feel that life-style is one of the important elements. In order to see this more clearly, we should consider a series of studies reported during the late 1960s. One study, of an Eskimo community in Barrow, Alaska, revealed what happens when a whole population changes its life-style. It reveals the price paid when a people changes from moving freely through open country and hunting for their food to becoming confined to houses and to a life in which survival primarily depends on passing the next written test. The findings of the study were grouped into three different age categories. The first consisted of the oldest members of the community. In this group almost nobody was found to be myopic. In the next age group, which involved the middle years, including women in the childbearing years, there suddenly appears a significant proportion of people who are myopic. This finding is contrary to most other studies of nomadic peoples, but interestingly enough, this study was conducted during the time when a dramatic shift was made in these Eskimos' way of life. This group of Eskimos lived a migratory life during their early childhood years until just shortly after World War II. Then they settled down to live in homes with plumbing, heat, electric lights, and television. School for some of them became compulsory. Diets were modified to include simple carbohydrates and sugars in great quantities. They changed to a "civilized" way of life and acquired many of civilization's ills—including myopia.

If the findings on this group reveal that a significant number were now myopic, what do you think the findings are on their children who grew up totally in this environment? The children's evaluations revealed that they are well on their way to completely reversing the findings of their grandparents. At the time of the study approximately 65 percent of the children were myopic. Give them another decade and perhaps the percentage of nearsightedness in children will equal the percentage of normal farsightedness that was found in their grandparents—an almost complete reversal in just two generations.

Barrow, Alaska, is not the only place where this change has occurred. There are at least four other studies that have revealed similar changes. They are studies of Eskimo populations in Alaska, the Canadian Northwest Territories, the Canadian eastern areas, and Greenland. One begins to wonder: What is the price of becoming civilized? What are the special conditions that bring about this maladaptation of our eyes?

In order to understand what causes our eyes to maladapt, let us look at the results of animal studies that have been in progress since at least 1950. In one series of studies, rhesus monkeys were confined to cages where they could not focus their eyes past approximately 12 inches. A control group of monkeys were in cages that allowed them to shift their focus to a far distance. After several months both groups were examined. About 75 percent of the animals that were not able to relax the focus of their eyes in order to see in the distance became myopic. The control group, on the other hand, did not become myopic.

The next study explored some of the reasons for this change. The pressure in the vitreous humor in the back of the monkeys' eyes was monitored during the experiment. When the experimental monkeys focused their eyes at a far-distant object, the pressure was recorded as normal. However, when the target was brought closer, the pressure increased in direct proportion to the closeness of the target. Each small increase in eye focus resulted in an increase in ocular pressure. An interesting side note to the experiment was when the examiners projected targets onto a screen for the monkeys to look at. Normally at that distance the animals would not need to use any focusing effort. However each time the examiners projected an image that was important to the monkey being tested, the pressure in its eye increased *as if* the target were brought closer.

These experiments show us the physiological requirements for the development of myopia. When you try to look at something at a close distance, the focusing muscle responds in order to maintain a clear view. As this occurs, the pressure elevates in the back of the eye. This is also true if you look at a distant target (such as a book) that is of extreme importance to you. The intensity effect increases the pressure above what would be usual for that distance. Although this is the way the human eye is made to work, what is *not* part of this design is the *continuous focusing of your eyes when you are intense or anxious.*

What this does is condition the focusing system to remain in a state of increased tension. The more a person remains in this situation, the more the body mobilizes its resources to maintain it.

Vision is not merely a passive event; it is a total body phenomenon. Everything we pay attention to is controlled by mental activity and is registered in the body's actions. Changes occur not only in the eye but throughout the body. As we become involved in an important task, brain activity shifts toward a goal orientation—reasoning and planning. Instead of seeing in a relaxed way and taking in a large panorama, an attitude of vigilance invests the person. This results in seeing details more acutely; however, attention is directed to only a small portion of the visual field. In the end, the person has to work harder because he observes less, sees less, and remembers less. Now the need is for categorization and concentration in the more concrete details of the experience. A different brain area becomes activated. There is an increase in arousal. As the nervous system becomes more aroused, different areas of the visual field are isolated for attention. This allows for an increase in the resolution of details. The patient's attitude of vigilance becomes fixed throughout the activity and sometimes long afterward. With the increase in vigilance come changes in breathing, heart rate, blood flow, pupil size, and galvanic skin response. In order to control what is perceived, emotional centers become involved. Nutritional and metabolic balances are continually altered as a part of this new involvement.

And this brings us to some research that is very new. If what I have mentioned so far were the whole story, optometrists probably would not see as many myopic patients showing destructive tissue changes. Many myopic patients would have a conditioned response of the muscles of the eye which is often reversible. However, the most destructive part of myopia is when the protective shell of the eye loses some of its elasticity and stretches. This is how one develops the elongated eye depicted so frequently in textbooks.

Over the years there have been many theories about the causes of myopia. Some have felt that the eyeball grew too large and thus left the person shortsighted. The image, in effect, focused short of the retinal screen. Others felt that the eye muscles were too tense. There have been reports that myopia was due to excessive close work, poor illumination, or psychological problems. Occasionally it seems that poor diet is the cause. All these explanations were probably right to some extent but only represented a small part of the problem. The picture we have now is perhaps somewhat more complete. But don't be surprised if research adds significantly to it in the years to come.

In order to understand this next part of our picture we have to view the eye as a fluid vessel housed in a tissue called the sclera. The vessel maintains a constant internal pressure. This pressure changes as we readjust our eyes from one distance to another. When we look at a distance beyond 15 feet the pressure is at a normal level of approximately 10 to 20 millimeters of mercury, as measured by an instrument called a tonometer. As we shift our focus to a closer distance, the pressure increases. The usual increase is between 5 and 10 millimeters of mercury. The increase appears many times each day and does not appear to be injurious to the eye. As a matter of fact, research has shown that squinting your eye can increase the pressure to approximately 110 millimeters of mercury, while rubbing your eye can elevate the pressure to 150 millimeters. So we can assume that increases in pressure ten times the norm are not harmful for the eye, provided they are momentary and occur in normal visual activities.

The sclera is a tissue made of a protein called collagen. This structural protein provides strength in virtually every connective, elastic, supportive tissue in the bodies of animals. Collagen is able to withstand large forces of applied pressures. But there is a point when it begins to give, and then irreversible stretching can occur. The major factor that pushes collagen beyond its elastic limits is sustained internal ocular pressure. And here we come to a brilliant discovery by a young researcher from New Jersey, Ben Lane. Dr. Lane's research has provided us with some very important missing links in the chain of events that leads to irreversible ocular change.

During the growth years from ages seven to seventeen, the

body needs calcium to support bone growth. In order to maintain an appropriate amount of tissue rigidity, collagen in the sclera also needs calcium. During these growth years, nature seems to have achieved a delicate balance. However, Dr. Lane's research shows how the development of myopia can upset this balance.

One of his first findings was that myopic patients had deficiencies of the trace mineral chromium. To be precise, young people increasing in myopia had one-third the level of chromium that nonmyopic patients had. Chromium is necessary in the process of converting foods into muscle energy, and it helps insulin in the work of glucose metabolism. It is released by the body into the bloodstream in response to the elevation of blood glucose. Following a meal heavy in refined sugars and carbohydrates—such as sweets, packaged cereals, or other processed items—an excess of chromium is released in order to aid metabolism. What chromium is not used is discharged into the urine.

In the eye, chromium is necessary to enable the uptake of glucose fuel for the ciliary muscle. The ciliary muscle is responsible for the eye's ability to shift and sustain its focus. When the available chromium is low, greater focusing effort must be applied. This in turn leads to an increase in the internal ocular pressure. Diets that are heavy in refined sugar and carbohydrates lead to chromium deficiencies. This may be why so many children today have focusing difficulties. Sometimes these focusing difficulties reduce the ciliary muscle's efficiency, and we then see what is called pseudomyopia. This is a spasm of the ciliary muscle. The patient spends long hours focusing at a close distance and then has difficulty shifting focus to farther distances. In effect, the distance view is blurred, but there is no change in the supporting tissue of the eye. The focusing muscle is unable to readjust. It is as if it has been conditioned to maintain a near focus. In the very beginning of this stage the patient may notice some inertia—a slow readjustment of the focusing mechanism as he looks up from his book. Some people report that the distance scene is blurred until they blink. This is the very early stage of the focusing spasm. In order to progress to tissue distension, the pressure in the eye must be maintained continuously and the scleral tissue itself must be weakened.

And so we come to Dr. Lane's next finding: that myopic patients have lost high amounts of calcium, as indicated by examining samples of their hair. A careful study of their diets reveals why. It seems that myopic patients in the growth years ingest a higher amount and a higher ratio of simple (refined) carbohydrates than patients not developing myopia. Patients not developing myopia had a ratio of approximately 10 percent refined to overall carbohydrates, while patients developing myopia consumed 35 percent of the carbohydrate intake as refined carbohydrates. This means that they take in fewer trace minerals (such as chromium) and fewer vitamins. Moreover, patients developing myopia ate three times as much flesh protein as their nonmyopic counterparts, who are not increasing in myopia. At first glance this high protein appears to be a benefit and not a disadvantage. However, we must take into account the many complex interactions of nutrients and other substances in the body. According to Dr. Lane, the high phosphorus content of animal protein stimulates the release of parathyroid hormone, a regulator of blood calcium levels which causes calcium to be drawn out of the scleral tissue and bone. (This not only weakens the sclera but it also results in reduced excitability of the ciliary muscle.) The calcium is then excreted in the urine or else winds up in the patient's hair. (It seems that the more calcium appearing in the hair, the less calcium available for tissue strength.) The end result is distension and contraction of the sclera.

Clearly, good nutrition plays an important role in the maintenance of healthy vision. But good nutrition is not enough. We also need a healthy attitude toward achievement. Slowly, we are beginning to see the subtle changes that civilization has wrought in our nation's health. If we can begin again to pay attention to what our bodies are saying, then perhaps we can change those conditions that affect the health of our children.

SOME SUGGESTIONS FOR MAINTAINING HEALTHY VISION

A. Nutrition
1. Eat lots of raw and fresh vegetables.
2. Avoid foods that have sugar added to them.
3. Reduce the amount of refined carbohydrates eaten.
4. Eat foods that supply rich sources of vitamins B_1, B_2, B_3, B_6, B_{12}, D, calcium, and chromium.
5. Obtain proteins from plant as well as animal sources.

B. Lighting
1. Make sure that there is no glare reflected from your reading materials.
2. Make sure that wherever reading is to be performed there is some general overhead lighting so that the surrounding field of vision is not totally dark. It should be about one-third the light level of the book.
3. The light falling on your reading material should come from a 150–200 watt source which is not farther than 3 feet from the reading material.

C. Posture
1. Always sit when reading.
2. Keep your whole body relaxed, not tense.
3. The distance that each eye should be from reading material is about the same as that between your elbow and the middle knuckle of your hand.

D. Time Limits
Never read for longer than 20 minutes. (For the average child this amounts to approximately 10 pages.) At the end of this period look up and focus your eyes on an object at least 15 to 20 feet away. You should be able to see it as clearly as you did before you began to read. If your vision remains unclear, stop reading and rest your eyes or do some simple visual focusing exercise.

E. Relaxed Attentiveness
1. Whenever you are concentrating for long periods of time try to make sure that your body does not tense up. Make sure that your breathing does not become constricted.
2. Try to become aware of the events around you without becoming distracted.
3. Every so often (1 hour) stand up and stretch your body. Next time you see a cat watch how he stretches.

F. Stress Relieving Lenses
About 80 percent of the people who are students or who read for long periods of time can benefit from using a special prescription for reading. Ask your optometrist to perform the functional near-vision tests that will determine if you could benefit from this form of optical protection.

G. Vision Therapy
If your eyes do not work efficiently when you read, then they are liable to rebel, causing headaches, eye strain, and

other symptoms that are associated with using your eyes for close, sustained tasks. The effort to compensate for the visual inefficiency can lead to visual distortions, such as myopia and astigmatism.

Your optometrist can prescribe therapy to develop the visual efficiency that you need for continued studying. The vision therapy that he prescribes is not a series of muscle exercises. It is a designed series of activities that allows you to unlearn faulty visual habits and develop new methods that will allow you to read without stress.

H. Outdoor Activities

Make sure that a good part of your week is spent outdoors, enjoying some healthy activities. These allow you to make use of your body and to have the opportunity to focus your eyes at far-distant objects.

Visual functions play a leading role in the developmental psyche of the infant.

—A. Gesell

STRABISMUS (EYE TURNS)

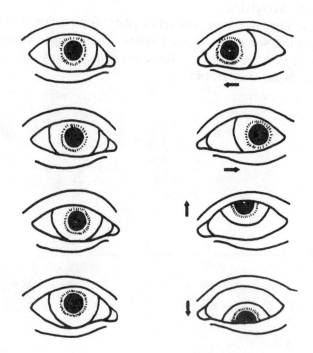

Strabismus

Strabismus is essentially a distortion of binocularity—the skill of getting the two eyes to work together as one shifts attention around the visual environment. Not only must the two eyes aim at the same object at the same time, but it is also necessary that the two messages, one from each eye, be integrated into one composite image. This is how we perceive three-dimensional depth and build up a knowledge of the relationships of ourselves to other objects in our environment.

In approximately 2 to 4 percent of the population this important skill does not develop completely, and then we have the condition known as strabismus, sometimes referred to as crossed eyes or walleyes. Although many people think that children are born with strabismus, studies have shown that this is not true. The most frequent age for strabismus to occur is between eighteen months and five years, with a large number of cases occurring between ages two and a half and three and a half.

If you notice that your child's eyes don't work together, you are likely to hear the same comments from professionals from whom you seek advice. One typical comment is that the child will grow out of it. Unfortunately, this is a damaging piece of advice. Built into the child's developmental growth plan is the development of two eyes, which year by year become more sophisticated in their working together and in their guiding the child's movement in space. The need for an integrated binocular system is so great that the brain has sections reserved for information coming from both eyes. Other sections are reserved for information coming from one eye. If something interferes with the development of binocular vision, some of the brain tissue reserved for binocularity can be lost.

As a child's binocular system develops, it helps him to orient himself in space. Approximately 20 percent of the visual fibers of the retina do not go toward interpreting what it is we are looking at; instead, they bring their information to the body's balance system. Thus, the child is able to sort out information that tells him whether he is right side up or tilted. Visual information is then interpreted along with body signals in order to properly orient the person to his world. One of the unfortunate effects of strabismus is that it interferes with this integration. If affects the child's perception of reality and as a result has a negative effect on his reality testing—his constant exploring in order to develop a stable sense of who he is. This in turn could affect the development of his ego. If his reality testing is deficient, then his ability to experience himself as something that has predictability falters. This frequently leads to a reduced drive to explore the world and its possibilities. Waiting for the child to grow out of the condition merely ensures that he will more firmly grow inward or else that he will strike out belligerently. This becomes more evident as the child begins to socialize when he is in school at around age six.

Sometimes it appears that the child has indeed outgrown the turned eye. Unfortunately, although both eyes appear to be straight, the cosmetic position of the eyes masks a totally different problem. When the child has a turned eye, he finds he is looking in two different directions at the same time. One eye is attending to something he wants to see; the other eye is giving him information about something he has no interest in. It can be very confusing. It can look to him as if one person is sitting on top of another person. Or instead, he may see two objects that appear to be attached, although he knows that this cannot be true. This condition, known as diplopia, or double vision, is confusing and upsetting for a child. One way the unconscious mind has of dealing with this experience is to pretend that it doesn't exist. This results in ignoring the message from one eye. The ignoring process, called suppression, is actually an active neurological process. It is as if you turned off the light because you didn't want to see what was in the room. Unfortunately, visual information continues to attract attention, so you find that the light in the room frequently comes on by itself. This means that you constantly have to turn it off. After a while the switch gets worn and doesn't work as well. By analogy, the visual suppression process leads to a reduced ability to see through the suppressed eye, even if you use the eye by itself. This is amblyopia ("lazy eye"), in which the nerves that interpret optical information have lost some of their interpretive ability. The result is poor vision in one eye. Because this is an interference in the neurological interpretive mechanism, it cannot be corrected with glasses or with surgery.

This is frequently what happens when the child "outgrows" strabismus. His eyes may look good cosmetically, but along the way he has had to suppress vision so frequently in one eye that he has all but lost the ability to see with it. The whole problem of amblyopia could have been avoided had the child been taken for vision therapy when the turned eye was first noted. To wait for the child to outgrow the condition only ensures that he will grow into a more serious physical or emotional problem. Although later you may be able to change the position of your child's eyes with vision therapy or with surgery, you can never recover the lost vision with surgery alone or with glasses. Fortunately today there are vision therapy procedures that have been developed which can help recover at least part of the lost vision. This is true even in the late adult years. However, it would have been so much simpler for all concerned had the child been taken for treatment at the first sign of visual difficulty.

This brings me to the second problem that is most often encountered. A parent who seeks advice about a child's turned eye is frequently told that the only thing to do is to have ocular surgery. Not only is this advice incorrect and misleading, but it can be dangerous in ways we hadn't thought of before. Often the reason given for recommending surgery is that the child has one or two eye muscles that are too long or too short, too tight or too loose. Therefore, it is claimed, the surgeon must cut the muscle and reposition it, tighten it, or loosen it. In fact, relatively few cases of strabismus are due to faulty muscles. Surgery may therefore be entirely unjustified in many cases.

Most often strabismus is the result of an interference in learning how to use the two eyes. Binocular vision is a learned skill. There appears to be an inborn program and schedule for its development. However, the completion of the program requires that experience and correct use be fostered. There are many things that can act as obstacles. A child can be born with a cataract (a milky clouding of the lens). This interferes with the image received by the affected eye. Another obstacle can be the continual closing of one eyelid. Sometimes a head injury received during birth, as from an incorrect forceps procedure, can lead to disrupted binocular development. Most often, as I have said, the interference comes through a disturbance of the neural control centers or the ability to attend to and absorb information from both eyes.

Disturbances in the neural control centers occur with high fevers and childhood illnesses such as roseola or chicken pox. It is not unusual for parents to report that the eye turned soon after the child had one of these illnesses. Sometimes the neural interference occurs for hidden reasons. I believe this is a reason why studies have shown a relationship between the development of strabismus and the delay in the child's learning to sit, walk, talk, and control elimination functions.

It seems that the mind pays attention more fully to the working of the visual system between the ages of four months and six years (or, most critically, between four months and three and a half years). After that period the mind is more critically involved in other learning skills. A delay in neural growth or the protective covering of nerves may put binocular development out of phase with the concentrated attention necessary to convert the eye coordination skills into conditioned habit patterns. If visual habits are not firmly fixed, they are then more vulnerable to loss.

At times it appears that the difficulty results from a psychological trauma that interferes with the mind's ability to attend during those critical years. We see this when patients have lost a parent or have gone through some emotional trauma shortly before developing a strabismus.

Psychological Effects of Strabismus

The literature concerning strabismus is replete with comments on the psychological aspects of the condition. An early study of the psychological causes was the report of the treatment of one of Freud's patients, Anna O. Freud reported that Anna developed strabismus while she was nursing her dying father. As a result of her psychotherapy, the strabismus disappeared. Unfortunately, we have no knowledge of whether the elimination of the strabismus cosmetically left Anna with an amblyopia condition—a frequent consequence when the patient does not undergo vision therapy to correct faulty ocular patterns that have become a neurological habit.

Many psychological studies report that strabismus influences personality in immediate and long-term ways. One of the earliest changes that occurs is the relationship between a mother and her child. Interviews with mothers of strabismic children show that these mothers are highly anxious about their children's condition and its possible social effects. This is reflected in the strabismic child's higher level of anxiety. Other studies reveal that strabismic patients have difficulty handling their feelings. They distrust their own perceptions as well as their ability to handle themselves well in social situations. They also demonstrate difficulty in achieving proficiency in sports and in easily acquiring academic skills.

When I first started my practice, the commonly held belief was that the lack of self-esteem, the feelings of inferiority, and the withdrawal from social contact that strabismic patients experience were all related to the cosmetic appearance. As the eye straightened, these personality difficulties tended to melt away. I found this to be true almost all of the time. Then I noticed that the same personality changes occurred when I treated strabismic patients whose eyes appeared cosmetically straight. The eye turn was so small that it was not observable even to the trained practitioner. I subsequently noticed similar personality changes after treating nonstabismic patients with other types of vision problems involving convergence, fusion, or focusing. It dawned on me then that the cosmetic appearance was not really related to the personality changes.

Not too long ago a study revealed that strabismic patients have significantly more psychological problems than the average individual, but that they have the same frequency of psychological problems as do patients who have other types of visual difficulties such as myopia, astigmatism, or other binocular problems.

As people develop visual problems, they come to distrust their own perception of reality, especially if the problems occur during the time in childhood when they are learning to gain a sense of mastery over their environment.

This brings me to the hidden dangers of ocular surgery to correct strabismus. By ignoring the correction of faulty neurological habits, surgery tends to fix those habits more firmly. Thus, the patient is left with two eyes that are correct cosmetically but only one eye that functions. The other eye has, in effect, lost permanently its ability to see. You would think that if the cosmetic problem were corrected nothing further would happen. But in many cases the unconscious desire to use both eyes is so great that the mind tries again. Only this time the original problem is compounded by the surgical procedures. What often happens in this case is that the eyes are correct for a short period of time, but then go out of alignment again. This time the position of the eye can be opposite to the original turn. For example, the right eye may have previously looked toward the nose; now, after the operation, it may start drifting out toward the ear. Sometimes the other eye starts to turn. And sometimes the result is a drift of one eye upward or downward. Occasionally the patient reports double vision.

Unfortunately, attempting only surgery for a strabismic condition ignores other aspects of a child's development. Over the years I have seen many adults who had this surgery as children. They come to me with eyes that look straight but that are not being used together. When I've asked them why they want to be in a vision therapy program when there is no apparent cosmetic problem, they have difficulty explaining their motives. The most frequent comment is that something is missing, something is wrong, or they do not feel that they are complete.

It took a long time for me, as a therapist, to understand the depth and pervasiveness of these feelings. Most often these same patients came to me while undergoing psychotherapy. They felt they needed some additional treatment specifically related to their eyes. It was only after seeing many adults with this problem and listening to their reports of what they experience in their vision therapy that I began to see that surgery, at least the way it is performed today, is damaging to most strabismic people. I know many surgeons and feel very strongly that they are superbly skilled technicians. But it appears that one aspect of being a skilled surgeon is the need to bury deeply any empathy they have when they must practice their craft.

> It seems nearly impossible for a surgeon to respond to each of thousands of fearful occasions... by feeling the compassion each situation merits.

> —Mark Kramer

This need to focus critically on the mechanical aspects of their job while suppressing their empathy works against the strabismic patient. Strabismus occurs at a critical phrase of child development. It occurs just when a child is developing mastery of the self as an independent person. It occurs just when the child is learning to separate from his parents and to strike out on his own. The child is exploring his relationships with things and people in his environment outside the home. It interferes with his developing a predictable reality and a sense of trust in himself. It also occurs during a transitional phase of sexual development, when the child must begin to integrate his sexual impulses. All these things the child is struggling to master at a time when he has to deal with the confusion that is the result of strabismus.

Surgery at this point is not a welcome or helpful intrusion. It is instead the start of new and possibly more serious problems. To give you a feel for what happens as a result of surgery, I am going to quote liberally from a letter that one of my patients wrote concerning her experiences. The letter is representative of many of the feelings that I have heard expressed by adult patients that I have treated. The only modification that I would make is that these feelings have been expressed more frequently by women than by men. The reason for this is not fully understood at the present time.

Kindergarten. Patch over one eye. Constantly stared at as if they're afraid of me. Teacher announces to class not to approach me on my "blind" side.

The eye tests deserve a heading of their own. A long series of (to me) meaningless tests spanning 23 years. Never knew what they wanted of me. Sometimes I'd answer what I thought was desired. Half the time I couldn't tell what I saw, but I knew the person was always waiting for an answer. Tests to me are expectations and labels that stick.

The search—a blur. I saw many doctors who said it was hopeless, a young woman, an older man, others. They only looked at my eyes and spoke to my eyes. I, the person, was invisible.

Found Dr. X. He was life and death to me. He found that I had fusion at close range. He said that he could help me. He was friendly. I was overjoyed. I returned for a second visit. He treated me like a stranger and said he was wrong. I wept. Mommy yelled at him.

The operations. The first one I barely remember. I didn't even see my own doctor before the first operation. I was examined by a stranger. The only pain I remember was when Dr. Y peeled back the bandages to look a day or two after. I feel that I saw everything. I have a visual memory of my stay in the hospital. Mom read to me. Bought me chocolate-chip cookies. There was a month at home. I remember my first bicycle ride and being afraid of sports with balls.

Second operation. The doctor insisted I be partially awake. The long needle injected into my cheek as I watched. Excruciating pain. I fainted again and again. Lying down with my eyes open. I watched the tools come down to my eyes through the blur. I never cried out. (This makes me cry now as I write it.) My right eye was horrible because he encountered scar tissue. It took twice as long. I don't remember his ever consoling me or caring. He was businesslike. The pain was enormous. I was a specimen. An animal in a laboratory. The room was small and ugly. They left me in the hall before the operation. Conscious, as people walked by. I was naked during both operations; even though I was covered, I was naked in the worst possible way. Strapped in, vulnerable, watching an uncaring man cut up my precious body. Injure me.

All my life I felt that I have been raped, but I couldn't tell anyone because they would say, "Did one of those doctors rape you with other people in the room?" Well, of course not. A girl's relationship to sex and rape is not based on adult definition. It was not a sex act forced on me. But my body, unprotected, was molested. There was pain. There was a lack of control of the situation. Something was taken away from me. The man didn't care about my feelings or the aftermath.

I remember the first time I presented these findings to other health professionals. During the course of my presentation I read sections of my patient's letter. The tears just streamed down from my eyes. It was a shocking indictment of the callous treatment doctors sometimes give their patients. Modern medicine has performed miracle after miracle in the last two hundred years. Unfortunately, this has left patients with a sense of awe and an uncritical acceptance of the medical care they receive. It is time that ophthalmic surgeons critically looked at their education concerning the treatment of patients as people. The technical training is, as I have said, superb. However, I feel that the training in understanding patients' emotional needs has not been covered adequately.

To gain some insight into the surgeon's world I recommend that you read Mark Kramer's eye opening book *Invasive Procedures*, a year in the world of two surgeons. Kramer relates how one surgeon felt about a patient who had just died. "You've got to insulate yourself, he says. He observes symptoms, formulates diagnoses, plans the tactics of treatment. His interest is no broader than that."

This is not the first time that I have dealt with this issue. In 1977 I coauthored an article with a psychoanalyst outlining the conjoint treatment of patients with strabismus. The thrust of the article was that in order to deal with the patient's visual problem, we must consider more than the eye. We must consider the person and the person's feelings. In order to successfully treat the patient, we must see him or her as a total individual. One ophthalmic clinic in Lisbon appears to be working in the right direction. They have combined their services with a mental health center in order to treat not only the visual problem but the associated psychological problem as well.

There are at least three steps to the correction of this situation. First, we should not consider surgery as the method of first choice. We must try to retrain the patient so that full binocular vision can be restored. Only if retraining will not eliminate the cosmetic problem should we consider a surgical alternative. Second, a nationwide research project should be started to determine whether my preliminary findings concerning the emotional results of surgery are true of a broad enough population to warrant changes in the education of ophthalmic surgeons. If only a small percentage of patients demonstrate the psychological changes that I have noted (which I rather doubt), then drastic changes in the ophthalmic surgeon's education may not be warranted. However, parents should be warned of the possible emotional side effects of surgery performed on strabismic children. Finally, if surgery is to be undertaken, a course of vision therapy should be given before as well as after, to ensure that both eyes will function as they were designed to. (See chapter 13 on finding an optometrist who offers vision therapy.)

Vision therapy involves providing patients with procedures (visual experiences) that allow them to slowly unlearn inappropriate responses. Sometimes the procedures are implemented by use of sophisticated instruments (modified stereoscopes) and at other times they are more like games using "funny" glasses.

Vision therapy is not something that is done to the patient, it is a visual situation that has been arranged for the person in order to teach appropriate visual responses. It rarely involves any pain and is most often a fun experience.

HYPEROPIA (FARSIGHTEDNESS)

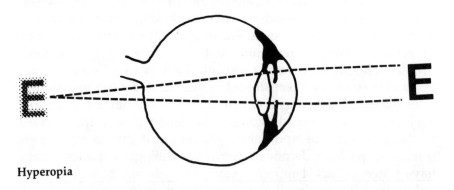

Hyperopia

If you were to have your baby's eyes examined shortly after birth, by several practitioners, you probably would receive different opinions concerning whether he was nearsighted or farsighted. You might even be told that one of his eyes was nearsighted while the other was farsighted. The opinion you receive would depend on the type of practitioner and his choice of examination method.

An examination requiring medication to immobilize your baby's focusing ability may lead the unwary practitioner to conclude that his measures indicate an unhealthy farsightedness. Similar conclusions can be drawn from examinations of infants who are asleep or drowsy. However, if that same child was examined in a normal, natural state, when he is actively looking at his surroundings, he will almost always reveal a healthier condition. It appears that the amount of farsightedness will vary with the state of alertness of the infant. In a medicated or drowsy state we will find him more unfocused or farsighted. When he is awake, curious, alert, and actively looking about, the measure of farsightedness found is usually small. This small amount is considered to be normal and perhaps even necessary.

If a large number of people around the world were examined, about 75 percent would be found to have some farsightedness. It appears, therefore, that statistically a small amount of farsightedness is the biologically normal state. This same pattern holds true for infants. The normal state of the eye of infants and children is a small amount of farsightedness, although slightly higher in amount than that measured after the age of eight.

Unfortunately, some children are born with an unhealthy amount of farsightedness. They are not able to adjust their visual systems to take in a sufficient level of information to guide their growth. As a result, they remain somewhat unfocused and uncritical in their behavior. We see this with children who have experienced neonatal anoxia (deficiency of oxygen reaching the tissues) or neonatal jaundice. We also see high amounts of farsightedness in retarded children.

There are children who have adverse amounts of farsightedness and have not experienced any harmful stress as newborns, nor are they retarded. It frequently appears that this form of farsightedness was created by prescribing glasses for infants at too early an age and of too great a correction. (The strength of the prescription does not allow the body to do some healthy adjusting.) This often occurs when the infant was examined in the medicated or unalert state, and the measurement was considered to be the final prescription without recourse to any further evaluation. Although glasses can be helpful for infants and children with strabismus or for those who are slow to focus on details, the prescription should allow the child some room to do his own focusing and not replace that skill or desire. When a prescription replaces a normal developmental function, the child may very well end up with an inability to exercise that function in a normal manner.

During the course of development the amount of farsightedness diminishes. The amount of farsightedness would almost appear to be an indirect measure of the child's alertness. As your child grows and shows interest in looking at and visually examining his world, he begins to reveal less farsightedness.

Several studies have shown that when a child looks at an object or a book with curiosity, his optical system reveals a small amount of farsightedness. When he becomes involved with its contents and begins to read their meaning (whether it is a picture or word seems to make no difference), the optical system begins to measure a small amount of nearsightedness. The optical measures shift back and forth between a small amount of farsightedness and a small amount of nearsightedness as the child demonstrates more or less involvement with the material.

Thus, the intensity of the focus seems related to the process of actively looking and making decisions about what is being looked at. I feel that this is the process that leads an infant to abandon his focusing daze. The physical and social environment entices the child to become involved with it and to focus on the various details that are offered. Slowly the child's farsightedness diminishes, until he is left with a small amount that we consider to be healthy.

This small amount of farsightedness tends to promote a need for alertness and a normal state of tension. This slight tension aids the healthy activity of muscles and blood flow. It is also considered healthy because it tends to act as a buffer or cushion during times of visual stress. Children who do not have this cushion and who are hyperalert and perhaps somewhat anxious tend to become nearsighted.

If your child is examined and the doctor reports a large amount of farsightedness that requires the constant wearing of glasses, make sure of the following:

1. The examination should have been performed when your child was not under the influence of medication, was not drowsy, and was visually alert.
2. The prescription should not fully neutralize your child's farsightedness unless he has an eye that turns in and the glasses help keep it straight, and unless the glasses are to be worn all the time for a predetermined period and not as a lifetime practice.
3. The doctor should reexamine your child regularly and try to reduce the prescription to allow him to function in a healthy manner more or less on his own.
4. The doctor should give you some suggestions or a program to visually stimulate your child. You should be provided with things to do that will require your child to continue to develop his visual alertness.

If your doctor does not believe that anything can be done to help your child except to provide a prescription that he will have to wear continuously for the rest of his life, I suggest that you get another opinion. Although a small number of children may have to follow this passive approach, the large majority can be helped to function in a healthier manner.

Look for a practitioner who has a background in child development and who understands how to promote normal healthy development. (See chapter 13.) Do not look for a technician whose only interest is in measuring the "exact" amount of farsightedness. Your child is not a camera. He is a living, growing person and needs to be treated as such.

ASTIGMATISM

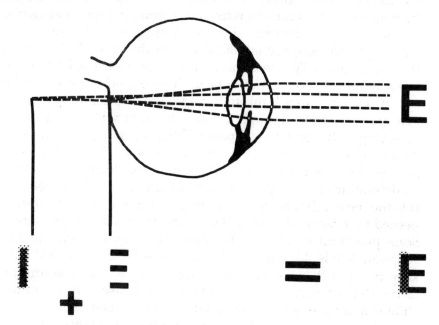

Hyperopic Astigmatism (Far-Sightedness)

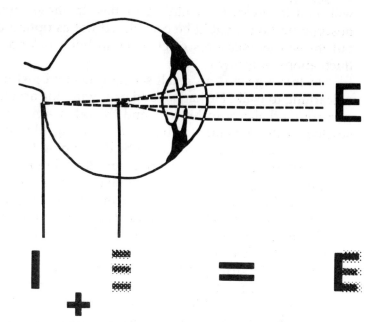

Myopic Astigmatism (Nearsightedness)

When your doctor examines your baby, one of the tests he will use is called retinoscopy. During this test he will shine a light from an instrument called a retinoscope into the baby's eyes while the baby is looking around. The retinoscope is really nothing more than a specially designed flashlight that lets the doctor look through the middle of the light beam as it enters the eyes. The back of the eye acts as a reflector. As the beam bounces off the back of the eye, it is reflected back through your child's optical system. It is like passing a light through a lens. The light will tend to focus according to the lens's focal power. This is also true for the eye. As the light is reflected back, it focuses according to the eye's focal power. The doctor, in effect, "reads" this focus. This is how he determines what type and strength of prescription is needed. It is the means that doctors have of determining the prescription needed for infants, retarded patients, and those who cannot speak. Some practitioners rely on this measurement for the ultimate prescription. While this may be necessary in some cases, you should keep in mind that the eye's focusing power will vary according to the state of alertness of the infant. It will also vary when the child is in a problem-solving situation or in a state of stress.

We frequently see this when examining infants who are struggling to coordinate their bodies. The retinoscope findings will tend to reveal the child's activities. In these cases the retinoscope findings should be considered not as optical distortions but instead as measures of changes in body balance related to fluctuations of growth.

In this regard I can recall seeing one child just in the stage of learning to walk. He had an odd gait, with one arm fairly active as a counterbalance to his legs and the other arm appearing restricted in its movement. There was nothing physically wrong with his arm. He appeared not to be developing the usual thrust and counterthrust of his arms and legs. An examination revealed an unusual astigmatic measure in one eye—the eye on the same side of the body as the restricted arm. My prescription was for some visual-motor games to stimulate more appropriate bilateral coordination. A later evaluation revealed that the unusual amount of astigmatism was reduced.

As a child struggles to coordinate his body, compensatory ocular reflexes adjust his eyes to maintain a relationship with the horizontal and vertical lines in his environment. If he bends his body to one side, his eyes tend to counter that change in body position by rotating in the opposite direction. As he does this, the eye muscles apply some tension to the eyeball. These adjustments may then be measured as an astigmatism. Some astigmatism therefore appears to be a measure of what your baby is doing to balance his body to gravity's pull.

The reader should be aware that this description will not be found when reading the usual definitions of astigmatism. The usual definition concerns itself with what is wrong with the eye. It usually suggests that it is "a defect of the eye or of a lens such that the rays of light from an object do not converge to form a focus, thus causing imperfect vision..."*

As an example of this, consider the astigmatic focus of a capital *E*. The horizontal lines would focus in a different place than the vertical line. This is why people with astigmatism occasionally confuse letters like *E*, *F*, and *T*.

The site of the discrepant bending power is usually thought of as the cornea, or front window of the eye. I have no argument with this definition if we want to look at the eye as an optical system and then determine what is wrong with it as an optical system. But I feel that we must always keep in mind that the eye is a living tissue attached to a thinking mind and frequently reflective of what the body is doing.

One of your baby's developmental tasks is to learn how to coordinate his body during different situations. This requires that he learn how to coordinate opposing muscle groups. As one set of muscles pulls, an antagonistic set of muscles must relax. It must do so just enough to support the action. Rarely is this task accomplished in one area of the body without other areas of the body taking part. It is as if the body were an orchestra, each part having a role to play in the ensuing symphony.

To get a feel for this interplay, just seat yourself comfortably on a hard, straight-backed chair. Be aware of your body sensations. Now shift your eyes to the extreme left and then to the extreme right. As you do this, you will notice that at a certain point you will feel a sensation in the neck area which is preparing to turn in support of your eye movement. Shortly you will feel your lower torso prepare itself for a body turn to support the head and eye movements. All of these sensations occur before the body

---

*Funk and Wagnalls Standard Desk Dictionary, Volume 1. New York: Funk and Wagnalls Inc., 1979.

actually moves. These supporting body shifts are often reflected in the eye's measures. During the early growth years it is not unusual to see these measurements fluctuate greatly, for they are primarily measurements of your child's developing visual-motor integration. Only when the measurements show continued repeatability over a period of at least one year should they be considered to be distortions of growth.

A prescription for this astigmatism would only be considered if the distortion is great enough to interfere with the clarity of your child's vision.

There are no doubt children who are born with an unusual amount of astigmatism that does not vary as they get older. When this astigmatism interferes with their learning to see, it should be dealt with early so that the child's visual development is not adversely affected. It is possible that this early unchanging astigmatism is related to cranial asymmetry or difficulties in birth. Whatever their cause, if they interfere with visual development, then a prescription is necessary to neutralize the results of the optical distortion.

Astigmatism due to the changes in visual-motor integration should not be neutralized at first with an optical prescription. The child should instead be given some visual-motor activities to help him develop better visual-postural abilities. Only if the astigmatism is interfering with development should an optical prescription be considered. Make sure that when your child uses his eyes for a concentrated period of time that he is free to move his eyes and head in all directions. Also, he should not constantly view objects off the midline of his body. Have him avoid drawing or studying with his head rotated or tilted. Visual games that stimulate free and easy coordination of eyes and head (such as a balloon catch) or eyes and body (such as climbing and hopscotch) should be used to offset long periods of coloring, drawing, or studying.

Your baby not only needs a doctor who is good at making accurate optical measurements; he also nees a person who understands how to support development in all of its variations and guises, as discussed in the next chapter.

13
Finding a Good Behaviorial Optometrist

Originally, the primary concern of optometrists was the measurement and fabrication of spectacles. Patients sought out optometric care because they could not see clearly. For some patients and some optometrists this remains the only service that is asked for and rendered even today. As knowledge in the eye-care field increased, optometric education began to change. Optometric educators recognized that knowledge about refraction (the measurement of the eye's imaging ability) by itself was not sufficient to help patients seeking eye care. The optometric curriculum was then expanded to include the diagnosis of ocular pathology and the diagnosis and treatment of functional visual problems. Optometrists began to recognize that the eye was more than a camera. It was living tissue—muscles and light-sensitive nerves—which were intimately connected to a thinking brain. Diagnostic and treatment procedures were then developed to ensure that patients were able not only to see clearly, but also to use their eyes in a comfortable manner. Visual evaluations began to include measurements of visual skills, such as the ability to move the eyes efficiently. Tests also evaluated the patient's focusing skills and binocular skills, such as fusion and eye aiming (convergence and divergence).

Many patients who had good visual acuity (clarity), but continued to report discomfort and confusion, were finally being helped. This change in optometric education and practice began to define optometric care as being uniquely different from ophthalmological care, which is more concerned with the treatment of ocular pathology (eye injuries and infections) and with the prescribing of spectacles for optical distortions.

During the early 1940s optometrists began to recognize that the visual skills they were treating had developed during the early childhood years. Research, especially the work of Dr. Arnold Gesell at the Gesell Institute of Child Development began to make clear the stages of vision development and the expected timetables for those developing skills. Optometrists such as Dr. Gerald Getman began to apply this knowledge to the treatment of retarded and brain-injured children. Optometric education again changed in a dramatic way. Optometrists educated themselves in the areas of child development, learning theory, and vision development. Many optometric practices began to reflect this change. Children with learning problems were finally finding an answer to their distress in optometric offices. Optometrists became skilled at giving developmental tests. These included many tests that were previously considered to be psychological or educational. However, optometrists began to reinterpret these tests to obtain information about vision development. New vision tests were also developed. These new concepts led to a better understanding of the patient's ability to interpret what he saw. Vision was then considered to be more than optical clarity or muscle and nerve functioning; it was seen as a learned skill that developed as the child developed and was influenced by what the child saw and did. Vision tests were then used to probe the level of the child's vision development as well as how the child used his vision to guide his actions and thoughts. The end result of the examination was to have a clear picture of the patient's vision, his comprehension of what he looked at.

At the present time, behavioral optometrists evaluate patients to make sure that their problems are not pathological or of optical origin. They evaluate the patient developmentally and also assess the effect that the patient's vision has on intellectual, emotional, social, and motor behavior. Behavioral optometrists recognize that behavior and vision have an effect on each other. At times the manner in which the visual system develops will influence the patient's behavior. At other times the patient's behavior—way of life, needs, and demands—may impose distortions on his vision.

This, then, is the present state of the practice of behavioral optometry. Some optometrists have fully committed themselves to practicing behaviorally, and others have elected to practice in the optical and functional areas primarily. How do you go about finding a good behavioral optometrist for your child?

The first step is to ask other health professionals for a recommendation. Do not overlook your own optometrist; discuss with him your search for a behavioral optometrist for your child. You might think that your pediatrician would be a good source; unfortunately, this has not always been the case in the past. Possibly this is true because their medical background emphasized the optical and pathological approaches to eye care. Some pediatricians however, are more sophisticated concerning child development and its relationship to learning and perception. By all means use your pediatrician as one source in your search, but don't forget the nursery school teacher, the dentist, the social worker, the psychologist, or any other professional that you or your family use. Professional people in a community get to know one another, and word gets around among them as to who is good with children.

Other good sources are your neighbors or the parents that you meet at school meetings, church or synagogue functions, community committees, and so on. A doctor who likes children and handles them well will soon be known by many parents.

Sometimes the Yellow Pages lists optometrists who specialize. I think that this is not a reliable enough source for you to use by itself, as some optometrists who practice in the way I have described do not call themselves behavioral optometrists. Most local optometric societies also maintain lists of practitioners who emphasize different areas of speciality. Lists such as these are also kept by the American Optometric Association, 700 Chippewa Street, St. Louis, Mo. 63119. However, most of the standard recommendations given from these lists are usually done on a rotating alphabetical basis with insufficient regard for qualifications. It would be better to contact the associations or schools that help educate practitioners in their specialities. The following is a list of sources in the United States and Canada.

OPTOMETRY SCHOOLS

Ferris State College
College of Optometry
Big Rapids, Mich. 49307

Illinois College of Optometry
3241 South Michigan Ave.
Chicago, Ill. 60616

Indiana University
School of Optometry
Indiana University
Bloomington, Ind. 47405

Inter-American University
of Puerto Rico
School of Optometry
G.P.O. Box 3255
San Juan, P.R. 00936

The New England College
of Optometry
424 Beacon St.
Boston, Mass. 02115

Northeastern State University
College of Optometry
Tahlequah, Okla. 74464

The Ohio State University
College of Optometry
338 West Tenth Ave.
Columbus, Ohio 43210
For information:
Department of Optometric
Assisting
Columbus Technical Institute
Mount Vernon Ave. at
Washington St.
Columbus, Ohio 43215

The Pacific University College
of Optometry
Forest Grove, Ore. 97116

Pennsylvania College
of Optometry
1200 West Godfrey Ave.
Philadelphia, Pa. 19141

Southern California College
of Optometry
2001 Associated Rd.
Fullerton, Calif. 92631

Southern College of
Optometry
1245 Madison Ave.
Memphis, Tenn. 38104

State University of New York
State College of Optometry
100 East 24th Street
New York, N.Y. 10010

University of Alabama
in Birmingham
School of Optometry/
Medical Center
University Station
Birmingham, Ala. 35294

University of California
School of Optometry
Berkeley, Calif. 94720

University of Houston
College of Optometry
4800 Calhoun
Houston, Tex. 77004

University of Missouri–
   St. Louis
School of Optometry
8001 Natural Bridge Road
St. Louis, Mo. 63121

University of Waterloo
School of Optometry
Waterloo, Ontario N2L 3G1

Ecole d'Optometrie
Université de Montreal
C.P. 6128
Succ. A
Montréal, Québec, Canada
   H3C 3J7

   If you are near an optometric school and can use its library, you might find *The Blue Book of Optometrists* a helpful source. It will give you information on optometrists' training and year of graduation, affiliations with continuing education facilities, areas of speciality, and so on.

   As more information has become available concerning developmental and behavioral aspects of vision, more optometrists have elected to practice behaviorally. Within the last decade it became necessary to establish two examining boards to provide a means of measuring competency in this speciality. Both make available to practitioners a mechanism for studying and then for being rigorously evaluated both academically and clinically. The evaluations provide a good means of determining competency in this new speciality. Both examining boards keep a list of optometrists who have successfully completed the examination process. If you write to them, they will let you know which optometrists in your area have successfully completed their evaluations in this speciality.

The Diplomate Program
   in Binocular Vision
   and Perception
The American Academy
   of Optometry
118 North Oak St.
Owatonna, Minn. 55060
(Optometrists who have
   completed this examination
   process are called
   diplomates.)

The College of Optometrists
   in Vision Development
353 H St., Suite C
Chula Vista, Calif. 92010
(Optometrists who have
   completed examinations are
   called fellows.)

Although the examination process sounds like a good idea, using these lists only would leave you without a source of very competent and creative optometrists who have not taken the time to apply for a diplomate or fellowship status. Excellent sources of continuing education have been available for optometrists since the early research in vision development began. Writing to obtain names of optometrists in your area would supply you with a list of practitioners who have continued deepening their knowledge of vision development and behavior. There are many optometrists who continually attend lectures and symposiums in order to keep their knowledge up to date. In your search, make sure that you include the following sources:

The Gesell Institute of
    Child Development
310 Prospect St.
New Haven, Conn. 06511

The Optometric Extension
    Program Foundation
2912 South Daimler St.
Santa Ana, Calif. 92705

You now should have a list of practitioners who have shown continuing interest in the area of child and vision development. They have spent considerable time increasing their knowledge by attending ongoing lectures and courses of study. Some have demonstrated their knowledge by taking very detailed examinations. You now have competence. It's time to see what your practitioner does with it and how you and your child like him or her as a person.

MAKING AN APPOINTMENT

When you call to make an appointment there are several things that you can find out besides the doctor's fees.

1. *How long will the examination last?* Any examination that lasts, on the first visit especially, less than a half an hour is not going to reveal more than the fact that your child has healthy eyes and whether or not he needs glasses. In order for the doctor to know whether your child's vision development is on track, a competent examination will run anywhere from forty-five minutes to two hours. The tests will include eye measurements as well as tests of motor coordination. Also included will be visual-motor and visual-perceptual tests. The type of tests used will depend upon your child's age.

2. *Does the doctor want any background information about your pregnancy and delivery and about your child's early developmental history?* If the answer appears to be that it is not necessary or important, you can rightfully question whether the doctor is concerned about protecting your child's vision development. Many practitioners will send out a history form to be completed and mailed back before the examination. Other doctors like to get the information at the time of the evaluation. Either way, the information is necessary to appreciate your child as a person and to be alerted to the effects of his early history.

3. *What kind of tests will the doctor administer?* For example, will there be tests to measure how your child's eyes work together—how they move, focus, and aim? Will the tests include measurements of how your child's visual system cooperates with his hands and body? Will tests be done to determine your child's level of visual perceptual development?

Whatever your child's age, there are tests that evaluate the degree of cooperation he has developed between his eyes, and between his eyes and hands. There are also tests that measure his understanding of what he sees. Each of these tests has age norms. As your child develops, the tests that will be used will be more sophisticated. Keep in mind that no child is too young for the doctor to obtain this information.

4. *What will the doctor do if he finds something wrong with your child's vision development?* If he feels that children outgrow vision immaturity problems or that the *only way* to handle *all* visual problems is to supply glasses, you are going to the wrong office. The doctor you want to see should be able to provide some guidance, some vision therapy, or some special therapy lenses in order to help your child grow properly. Occasionally a very young child will have an optical distortion that is interfering with his growth. In this case it is appropriate to use an optical correction. But if that is the only service available, go elsewhere. Sometimes you will find a very good diagnostician who prefers to refer children for the vision therapy that they need. I see nothing wrong with this arrangement, especially if he appears to really know your child and know his needs.

5. *Is the doctor willing to correspond with other professionals who will see your child?* This includes your pediatrician, your child's teacher, and perhaps any other professional you may want to see to help protect and aid your child's development. If the doctor says that he is too busy to send reports, then you will be missing

an important means of communicating your child's special needs. For many children the developing years present no unusual problems. However, many other children today experience visual and perceptual difficulties that interfere with their developing egos if they are not recognized and handled properly. For example, wouldn't it be better if a little girl's teacher knew about her eye-hand coordination problems and emphasized tumbling instead of playing ball? Her teachers also might provide help with the eye-hand coordination program that her optometrist has prescribed.

If you have to move to a new city, it is important to know that you don't have to start all over again. You will want to know if the doctor you select will help you to find someone to continue your child's care and that he will also supply any information that is needed.

6. *How does the doctor intend to follow up on your child's progress?* If his policy is to wait for your child to experience difficulty, or if he feels that evaluations every couple of years are sufficient, then you are talking to someone who does not practice preventive care. One of the main reasons to have your child evaluated early is to catch problems before they arise, or at least in their very earliest stages. In order to do this, the evaluations should be fairly regular. They should follow a sensible developmental timetable. For vision development the timetable should include a visit at age six months, at one year, at eighteen months, at two years, at two and a half years, three years, four years, and then yearly from that point on. If your child is receiving some treatment, then the evaluation schedule may be dictated by the therapy.

During the regular examinations the doctor will compare the results of previous examinations to detect any early deviations from what is expected. Therapy or guidance can then be applied at an early stage to make sure that a misstep in development does not end up as a permanent disability.

THE VISIT

Once you have gotten the right answers to your questions, it is time to take your child to the new optometrist and find out whether you will all get along with each other. The desirable qualities on the doctor's part involve liking children and being skillful in handling them. This includes not being too disturbed by any noise or mess they might make in his office. The evaluation should be child-oriented, using materials and procedures that will elicit the responses and answers needed to determine how and what your child sees. A child's lack of verbal skill should not be an obstacle to getting the information needed. Finally, it is very important that the optometrist can communicate to you, the parent, in a comprehensible fashion. It is not enough to know that your child has been evaluated properly; you should also have a clear understanding of your child's vision development and of his needs.

When you have finally found the right optometrist, make sure you share him or her with a friend.

Bibliography

CHAPTERS 1–4

Ames, Louise, and Ilg, Frances. *Your Two Year Old*. New York: Delacorte Press, 1976.

Ames, Louise, and Ilg, Frances. *Your Three Year Old*. New York: Delacorte Press, 1976.

Ames, Louise, and Ilg, Frances. *Your Four Year Old*. New York: Delacorte Press, 1976.

Apell, R. and Lowry, R. *Preschool Vision*. St. Louis: American Opton Association, 1959.

Ayres, Jean. *Sensory Integration and the Child*. Los Angeles: Western Psychology Services, 1979.

Bower, T. G. R. *A Primer of Infant Development*. San Francisco: W.H. Freeman & Co., 1977.

Bower, T. G. R. *The Perceptual World of the Child*. Cambridge: Harvard University Press, 1977.

Braga, Laurie, and Braga, Joseph. *Learning and Growing*. New Jersey: Prentice-Hall, 1975.

Cannon, Walter. *The Wisdom of the Body*. New York: W.W. Norton & Co., 1939.

Dileo, Joseph. *Young Children and Their Drawings*. New York: Brenner-Mazel, 1970.

Eliot, John, and Salfund, Neil. *Children's Spatial Development*. Springfield: Charles C. Thomas, 1975.

Flavell, J. *The Developmental Psychology of Jean Piaget*. New York: D. Van Nostrand Co., 1963.

Fraiberg, Selma. *Insights from the Blind*. New York; Basic Books Inc., 1977.

Gesell, A., Ilg, Frances, and Ames, Louise. *Infant and Child in the Culture of Today*. New York: Harper & Row, 1943.

Gesell, Arnold, Ilg, Frances, and Bullis, Glenna. *Vision: Its Development in Infant and Child*. New York: Paul B. Holber Inc. Medical Book Dept. of Harper and Bros., 1949.

Gesell, A. et al. *The First Five Years of Life*. New York: Harper & Row, 1940.

Green, Philip, and Gordon, Michael. "Maternal Deprivation: Its Influence on Visual Exploration in Infant Monkeys." *Science*, Vol. 145 (July 17, 1962), p. 292.

Hall, Edward. *The Hidden Dimension*. New York: Avelrob Books, 1966.

Jackson, Jane, and Jackson, Joseph. *Infant Culture*. New York: Plume—New American Library, 1978.

Josselyn, Irene. *Psychosocial Development of Children*. New York: Family Service Association of America, 1948.

Kaplan, L. *Oneness and Separateness: From Infant to Individual*. New York: Touchstone Book—Simon & Schuster, 1978.

Kliman, Gilbert, and Rosenfeld, Albert. *Responsible Parenthood*. New York: Holt, Rinehart & Winston, 1980.

Kogan, Nathan. *Cognitive Styles in Infancy and Early Childhood*. New York: John Wiley & Sons, 1976.

McCall, Robert. *Infants*. New York: Vintage Books, 1980.

Montagu, M.F. Ashley. *The Direction of Human Development*. New York: Harper & Bros., 1955.

The Nature and Nurture of Behavior Developmental Psychology. Reading from *Scientific American*, San Francisco: W.H. Freeman & Co., 1972.

Orem, R.C. *Learning to See*. Johnson: Mafex Association, 1971.

Pulaski, Mary Ann. *Your Baby's Mind and How It Grows*. New York: Harper—Colophon Books, 1981.

Reisen, Austen. *The Developmental Neuropsychology of Sensory Deprivation*. New York: Academic Press, 1975.

Sime, Mary. *A Child's Eye View.* New York: Harper & Row, 1973.

Spitz, René. *The First Year of Life.* New York: International University Press, 1965.

Stern, D. *The First Relationship.* Cambridge: Harvard University Press, 1977.

White, Burton. *The First Three Years of Life.* New Jersey: Prentice-Hall, 1975.

Willemsen, E. *Understanding Infancy.* San Francisco: W.H. Freeman & Co., 1979.

CHAPTER 5

Ames, Louise, Gillespie, Clyde, and Streff, John. *Stop School Failure.* New York: Harper & Row, 1972.

Bateman, Barbara, editor. *Learning Disorders.* Seattle: Special Child Publisher, 1971.

Clarke, Louise. *Can't Read Can't Write Can't Talk Too Good Either.* New York: Walker & Co., 1973.

Critchely, Macdonald. *The Dyslexic Child.* London: William Heineman Medical Books, 1964.

Crow, Gary. *Children at Risk.* New York: Schocken Books, 1978.

Flapan, Dorothy, and Newbauer, Peter. *Assessment of Early Child Development.* New York: Jason Aronson Inc., 1975.

Greenstein, Tole, editor. *Vision and Learning Disability.* St. Louis: American Optometric Association, 1976.

Hallahan, Daniel, and Kauffman, James. *Introduction to Learning Disabilities.* New Jersey: Prentice-Hall, 1976.

Harris, Albert, and Sipay, Edward. *How to Increase Reading Ability.* New York: David McKay, 1940.

Jones, Beverly, and Hart, Jane. *Where's Hannah?* New York: Hart Publishing Co., 1968.

Jordan, Dale. *Dyslexia in the Classroom.* Columbus: Charles E. Merrill, 1972.

Kephart, Newell. *The Slow Learner in the Classroom.* Columbus: Charles E. Merrill, 1960.

Levine, M., Brooks, R., and Shonkoff, J. *A Pediatric Approach to Learning Disabilities.* New York: John Wiley & Sons, 1980.

Levy, Harold. *Square Pegs Round Holes.* Boston: Little, Brown & Co., 1973.

Painter, Genevieve. *Teach Your Baby*. New York: Simon & Schuster, 1971.

Quiros, Julio, and Schrager, Orlando. *Neuropsychological Fundamentals in Learning Disabilities*. Novato: Academic Therapy Pub., 1978.

Rosner, Jerome. *Helping Children Overcome Learning Difficulties*. New York: Walker & Co., 1975.

Sapir, S., and Nitzburg, A., editors. *Children with Learning Problems*. New York: Brenner-Mazel, 1973.

Smith, Sendon. *Improving Your Child's Behavior Chemistry*. New Jersey: Prentice-Hall, 1976.

Solan, Harold, editor. *The Psychology of Learning and Reading Difficulties*. New York: Simon & Schuster, 1973.

Spache, George. *Investigating the Issues of Reading Disabilities*. Boston: Allyn & Bacon, 1976.

Spache, George. *Diagnosing and Correcting Reading Disabilities*. Boston: Allyn & Bacon Inc., 1976.

Waugh, Kenneth, and Bush, Wilma. *Diagnosing Learning Disorders*. Columbus: Charles E. Merrill, 1971.

Wold, Robert, editor. *Visual and Perceptual Aspects for the Achieving and Underachieving Child*. Seattle: Special Child Pub., 1969.

Wold, Robert, editor. *Vision: Its Impact on Learning*. Seattle: Special Child Pub., 1978.

Wunderlich, Ray. *Kids, Brains & Learning*. St. Petersburg: Johnny Reads Inc., 1970.

CHAPTER 6

Arena, John. *Teaching Through Sensory-Motor Experiences*. San Rafael: Academic Therapy Pub., 1969.

Piers, Maria. *Play & Development*. New York: W.W. Norton & Co., 1972.

Radler, D. H., and Kephart, Newell C. *Success Through Play*. New York: Harper & Bros., 1960.

CHAPTER 7

Charren, Peggy, and Sandler, Martin. *Changing Channels*. Reading: Addison-Wesley, 1983.

Kriegman, Herbert. "Brain Wave Measures of Media Involvement." *Journal of Advanced Research* (February 1971), pp. 3–9.

Liebert, Robert, Neale, John, and Davidson, Emily. *The Early Window Effects of Television on Children and Youth.* New York: Pergamon Press, 1973.

Loftus, Geoffrey, and Loftus, Elizabeth. *Mind at Play: The Psychology of Video Games.* New York: Basic Books, 1983.

Mander, Jerry. *Four Arguments for the Elimination of Television.* New York: William Morrow, 1978.

U.S. Dept. of Health and Human Services, National Institute for Occupational Safety and Health, Supt. of Documents. *Potential Health Hazards of Video Display Terminals.* Washington: U.S. Government Printing Office, June, 1981.

Wilkins, Joan. *Breaking the TV Habit.* New York: Charles Scribner's Sons, 1982.

Winn, Marie. *The Plug-in Drug.* New York: Viking, 1977.

CHAPTER 8

Anderson, James, and Cohen, Martin. *The Competitive Edge.* New York: Bantam Books, 1981.

Burke, Miles. "Soccerball-Induced Eye Injuries." *JAMA*, Vol. 249, No. 19 (May 20, 1983).

Cooper, Donald. "Physical Examination and Primary Care of the Young Athlete." *Sports Medicine Digest*, Vol. 3, No. 8 (August, 1981).

Faulkner, Edwin, and Weymuller, Frederick. *Tennis: How to Play It, How to Teach It.* New York: Dial Press, 1970.

Muse, Bill. *We Can Teach You to Play Soccer.* New York: Hawthorn Books, 1976.

Schneider, Steven. "Flex Your Eyes." *Washington Post Magazine* (Sept. 18, 1983).

Seiderman, Arthur, and Schneider, Steven. *The Athletic Eye.* New York: Hearst Books, 1983.

Shephard, Roy. *Physical Activity and Growth.* Chicago: Yearbook Medical Pub., 1982.

CHAPTER 9

Davis, Adelle. *Let's Have Healthy Children.* New York: Signet Books, 1972.

Krause, M., and Mahan L. *Food, Nutrition and Diet Therapy.* Philadelphia: W.B. Saunders, 1979.

Smith, Lendon. *Foods for Healthy Kids.* New York: Berkley Books, 1981.

Smith, Lendon. *Feed Your Kids Right.* New York: Dell, 1979.

Wynder, E., editor. *The Book of Health.* New York: Franklin Watts, 1981.

CHAPTER 10

Crow, Gary. *Children at Risk.* New York: Schocken Books, 1978.

Hirsch, M., editor. *Vision of Children.* Philadelphia: Chilton Books, 1963.

Levine, M., Brooks, R., and Shonkoff, J. *A Pediatric Approach to Learning Disabilities.* New York: John Wiley & Sons, 1980.

Riesen, Austen. *The Developmental Neuropsychology of Sensory Deprivation.* New York: Academic Press, 1975.

Spitz, René. *The First Year of Life.* New York: International University Press, 1968.

Wunderlich, Ray. *Kids, Brains, & Learning.* St. Petersburg: Johnny Reads, 1970.

CHAPTER 11

Helmuth, J., editor. *Exceptional Infant—The Normal Infant.* New York: Brunner-Mazel, 1967.

Henderson, John. *Emergency Medical Guide.* New York: McGraw-Hill, 1978.

Samuels, Mike, and Samuels, Nancy. *The Well Child Book.* New York: Summit Books, 1982.

Samuels, Mike, and Samuels, Nancy. *The Well Baby Book.* New York: Summit Books, 1979.

CHAPTER 12

Baldwin, William. "A Review of Statistical Studies of Relations Between Myopia and Ethnic, Behavioral and Psychological Characteristics." *American Journal of Optometry and Physiological Optics* (Vol. 58, No. 7, July 1981), pp. 516–527.

Beach, G., and Kavner, R. "Conjoint Therapy: A Cooperative Psychotherapeutic-Optometric Approach to Therapy." *Journal of The American Optometric Association* (December 1977), pp. 1501–1507.

Bonsor, A. "Some Comments on the Question of Early Operation." *British Optometric Journal* (Vol. 16, 1959), pp. 114–118.

Burnbaum, Martin. "Clinical Management of Myopia." *American Journal of Optometry & Physiological Optics* (Vol. 58, No. 7, July 1981), pp. 554–559.

Butti, G. "Problems of Anesthesia in Strabismus Surgery." *International Ocular Clinics*, 6 (1966).

Daubs, J., and Shotwell, Alan. "Optical Prophylaxis for Environmental Myopia: An Epidemiological Assessment of Short-Term Effects." *American Journal of Optometry and Physiological Optics* (Vol. 60, No. 4, April 1983), pp. 316–320.

Dunlap, E. "Complications in Strabismus Surgery." *International Ocular Clinics*, 6 (1966).

Gartner, S., and Billet, B. "A Study of Mortality Rates During General Anesthesia for Ophthalmic Surgery." *American Journal of Ophthalmology* (Vol. 45, Nov.), pp. 847–849.

Greene, Peter. "Mechanical Considerations in Myopia: Relative Effects of Accommodation Convergence, Intraocular Pressure and the Extraocular muscles." *American Journal of Optometry and Physiological Optics* (Vol. 57, No. 12, Dec. 1980), pp. 902–914.

Greenspan, Steven. "Research Studies of Bifocals for Myopia." *American Journal of Optometry and Physiological Optics* (Vol. 58, No. 7, July 1981), pp. 536–540.

Hoffman, L., Cohen, A., Fener, G., and Klayman, I. "Effectiveness of Optometric Therapy for Strabismus in a Private Practice." *American Journal of Optometry & Archives of the American Academy of Optometry* (Vol. 47, Dec. 1970), pp. 508–518.

Kavner, R., and Suchoff, I. *Pleoptics Handbook.* New York: State University Press, 1972.

Kramer, Mark. *Invasive Procedures.* New York: Harper & Row, 1979.

Ku, David, and Greene, Peter. "Scleral Creep In Vitro Resulting from Cyclic Pressure Pulses: Applications to Myopia." *American Journal of Optometry and Physiological Optics* (Vol. 58, No. 7, July 1981), pp. 528–535.

Lane, Ben. "Chromium and Accommodative Weakness." *Proceedings of International Society for Eye Research* (Vol. I, 1980), pp. 72–73.

Lane, Ben. "Calcium, Chromium, Protein, Sugar and Accommodation in Myopia." In H.C. Fledelius, P.H. Alsbirk, and E. Goldschmidt (Eds.), Documents Opthalmoligica Proc. Series (Vol. 28, Third International Conference on Myopia). Copenhagen, The Hague: Dr. W. Junk Publishers, 1981, pp. 141–148.

Lane, Ben. "Myopia Prevention and Reversal: New Data Confirms the Interaction of Accommodative Stress and Diet-Inducing Nutrition." *Journal of the International Academy of Preventive Medicine* (Vol. VII, No. 3, Nov. 1982), pp. 17–30.

Layon, Richard, and Giddings, John. "Psychological Approaches to Myopia: A Review." *American Journal of Optometry and Physiological Optics* (Vol. 51, No. 4, April 1974), pp. 271–281.

Ludlam, William. "Orthoptic Treatment of Strabismus." *American Journal of Optometry & Archives of the American Academy of Optometry* (Vol. 38, July 1961), pp. 369–388.

Ludlam, William, and Kleinman, B. "The Long Range Results of Orthoptic Treatment of Strabismus." *American Journal of Optometry & Archives of the American Academy of Optometry* (Vol. 42, Nov. 1965), pp. 647–684.

Young, Francis. "The Effect of Restructured Visual Space on the Primate Eye." *American Journal of Ophthalmology* (Vol. 52, No. 5, 1961).

Young, Francis; Surger, Redmond; and Foster, Dean. "The Psychological Differentiation of Male Myopes and Non Myopes." *American Journal of Optometry and Physiological Optics* (Vol. 52, No. 10, Oct. 1975), pp. 679–686.

Young, Francis. "Primate Myopia." *American Journal of Optometry & Physiological Optics* (Vol. 58, No. 7, July 1981), pp. 560–566.

Index

alcohol, pregnancy and, 182
amblyopia ("lazy eye"), 208
American Alliance for Health,
    Physical Education, and
    Recreation and Dance, 147
American Optometric Association, 225
  Sports Vision Section of, 146
anesthetics, 181
anoxia, neonatal, 217
antibiotics, 179
antioxidants, 171
Apgar scores, 184
Armstrong, Neil, 74
aspirin, 179
astigmatism, 219–22
  bilateral coordination and, 221–22
  correction of, 222
  definition of, 220–21
  diagnosis of, 220
attention problems:
  learning disabilities and, 97
  reciprocal body control and, 82

saccadic eye-movement skills and,
    84

backaches, 86
ball-playing:
  binocularity and, 85, 86, 141–42
  eye-hand coordination and, 103
  eye-tracking ability and, 83, 103
  see also play; sports
BHA, 171
BHT, 171
bilateral coordination, 99
  astigmatism and, 221–22
  developmental lags in, 105–6
  in five year olds, 106
  in four-to-eight month olds, 105
  in four year olds, 74–75, 106
  learning and, 99
  in newborns, 105
  in nine-to-eighteen month olds,
    105

DR. RICHARD S. KAVNER received his doctorate in Optometry from the Massachusetts College of Optometry. He is a former consultant to the New York City Board of Education District #11, And a former chairman of The Vision Training Department of the Optometric Center of New York. Dr. Kavner has been chairman of the Sports Vision Section of the American Optometric Association, and has conducted a vision program at the Nation Sports Festivals. He is a Fellow of the American Academy of Optometry, from which he was awarded Diplomate status in Binocular Vision and Perception. Dr. Kavner's practice is in New York City.